Madhur Jaffrey
Indian Cookery

Madhur Jaffrey
Indian Cookery

BBC

notes on the recipes

- Eggs are medium unless stated otherwise
- Wash all fresh produce before preparation
- Spoon measurements are level
- Conversions in the recipes are approximate and have been rounded up or down. Follow one set of measurements only; do not mix metric and imperial

LIQUID CONVERSIONS

1 tablespoon = 15 ml or 3 teaspoons

1 teaspoon = 5 ml

metric	imperial	US
10 ml	2 tsp	2 tsp
20 ml	1 tbsp	1½ tbsp
30 ml	1 fl oz	2 tbsp
60 ml	2 fl oz	¼ cup
125 ml	4 fl oz	½ cup
185 ml	6 fl oz	¾ cup
250 ml	8 fl oz	1 cup/½ pint
300 ml	10 fl oz/½ pint	1¼ cups
500 ml	16 fl oz	2 cups/1 pint
575 ml	20 fl oz/1 pint	2½ cups
1 litre	35 fl oz/1¾ pints	4½ cups

DRY/OTHER CONVERSIONS

As a general guide, regard 2 US teaspoons or tablespoons as 1 UK teaspoon or tablespoon.

1 dessertspoon is the equivalent of 2 teaspoons or half a tablespoon.

commodity	metric	imperial	cups
Butter/margarine	225 g	8 oz	1 cup
Breadcrumbs	90 g	3¼ oz	1 cup
Cheese (cheddar, parmesan etc. grated)	50 g	2 oz	1 cup
Dried fruit (raisins, sultanas etc.)	225 g	8 oz	1 cup
Flours (finely ground)	15 g	4 oz	1 cup
Coarse meals (semolina, oatmeal etc.)	40 g	5 oz	1 cup
Nuts (almonds, hazelnuts, walnuts etc.)	150 g	5½ oz	1 cup
Ground nuts	115 g	4 oz	1 cup
Rice (uncooked)	115 g	4 oz	1 cup
White sugar	225 g	8 oz	1 cup
Brown sugar	170 g	6 oz	1 cup
Icing sugar	40 g	5 oz	1 cup
Treacle/syrup	350 g	12 oz	1 cup

preface

Nothing is more gratifying for any author than to have a book that has sold consistently well for over 20 years. Many young people come up to me today and say that they grew up on my food, cooked for them by their parents and that they are now cooking from my books for their children. It is enough to move me to tears.

When it was decided to do this latest 'update' with fresh photographs, I found myself looking at my recipes again to see if they needed revising. They don't. They work just as well today as they did when I wrote them. What has changed is the world around us.

The day after I cooked Lemony Chicken with Fresh Coriander (page 95) on television in the 1980s, I was told that Manchester ran out of green coriander. This would not happen today. Even our supermarkets now are stocked with everything from fresh ginger and green chillies to okra. Basmati rice is sold universally, often in handy bags with zips, all cleaned and ready to go. Fully cooked *naans*, packaged to ensure freshness, can be had in Britain from the neighbourhood grocer to accompany a home-cooked Rogan Josh (page 70). Spice companies sell whole cumin and whole red chillies. This fills me with joy.

Even kitchen gadgets have moved along. It had been my dream to make a Japanese-style grater, perfect for ginger, universally available. It did not happen. Never mind. We now have the microplane grater. Fresh ginger moves on it like butter, providing a perfect 'paste'. You can even use it for large cloves of garlic. Garlic cloves have grown in size, haven't they? The little bits that are left can be collected and pushed through a garlic press. Cooking is becoming so much easier.

As the pace of life gets faster, many of us are turning, in our leisure hours, to ancient disciplines that help slow it down and give it perspective. Ayurveda is one of them. It tells us that simple kitchen acts like chopping, cutting and grinding are graces that help calm the soul and bring it closer to its origins. Is that not what we are all searching for? Some think so.

When I first wrote *Indian Cookery*, Indian food was available mostly in second-rate restaurants at relatively cheap prices and considered the perfect accompaniment to mugs of beer or lager. While this is still true, two other things have happened. There is a better grade of restaurants, many serving regional foods, that have appeared, selling freshly cooked specialities. Also, there is a whole new generation of people cooking Indian food at home, from simple breakfast eggs to elaborate legs of lamb. They know better and are both knowledgeable and demanding. They may have gone to culinary schools. They may have travelled to India or have cookery books to guide them. They are not easily fooled. They want authentic food. Good ingredients, properly cooked. This book is dedicated to them.

Madhur Jaffrey

introduction

I have always loved to eat well. My mother once informed me that my passion dates back to the hour of my birth when my grandmother wrote the sacred syllable 'Om' ('I am') on my tongue with a finger dipped in fresh honey. I was apparently observed smacking my lips rather loudly.

Starting from that time, food – good food – just appeared miraculously from somewhere at the back of our house in Delhi. It would be preceded by the most tantalizing odours – steaming basmati rice, roasting cumin seeds, cinnamon sticks in hot oil – and the sounds of crockery and cutlery on the move. A bearer, turbaned, sashed and barefooted, would announce the meal and soon we would all be sitting around the dinner table, a family of six, engrossed in eating monsoon mushrooms cooked with coriander and turmeric, *rahu* fish that my brothers had just caught in the Jamuna River, and cubes of lamb smothered in a yoghurt sauce.

It was at this stage of innocence that I left India for London, to become a student at the Royal Academy of Dramatic Art. My 'digs' were in Brent and consisted of a pleasant room and, through the kindness of my landlords, use of the kitchen.

'Use of the kitchen' was all very well, but exactly how was I going to use it? My visits to our kitchen in Delhi had been brief and intermittent. I could not cook. What was worse, I felt clumsy and ignorant.

An SOS to my mother brought in return a series of reassuring letters, all filled with recipes for my favourite foods. There they were, *Kheema matar* (Minced meat with peas), *Rogan josh* (Red lamb stew), *Phool gobi aur aloo ki bhaji* (Cauliflower with potatoes) …

Slowly, aided by the correspondence course with my encouraging mother, I did learn to cook, eventually getting cocky enough to invite large groups of friends over for meals of *Shahi korma* or *Shahjahani murghi* (Mughlai chicken with almonds and raisins). Once certain basic principles had been mastered, cooking Indian food had become perfectly accessible.

There is something so very satisfying about Indian cookery, more so when it is fresh and home-cooked. Perhaps it is that unique blending of herbs, spices, seasonings, as well as meat, pulses, vegetables, yoghurt dishes and relishes that my ancestors determined centuries ago would titillate our palates. At the same time it preserves our health and the proper chemical balance of our bodies. This combination of wholesome food and endless flavours and dishes makes Indian cookery one of the greatest in the world.

Indian food is far more varied than the menus of Indian restaurants suggest. One of my fondest memories of school in Delhi is of the lunches that we all brought from our homes, ensconced in

multi-tiered tiffin-carriers. My stainless-steel tiffin-carrier used to dangle from the handle of my bicycle as I rode at great speed to school every morning, my ribboned pigtails fluttering behind me. The smells emanating from it sustained me as I dodged exhaust-spewing buses and, later, as I struggled with mind-numbing algebra. When the lunch bell finally set us free, my friends and I would assemble under a shady *neem* tree if it was summer or on a sunny verandah if it was winter. My mouth would begin to water even before we opened up our tiffin-carriers. It so happened that all my friends were of differing faiths and all came originally from different regions of the country. Even though we were all Indian, we had hardly any culinary traditions in common. Eating always filled us with a sense of adventure and discovery as we could not always anticipate what the others might bring.

My Punjabi friend was of the Sikh faith. She often brought large, round *parathas* made with wheat and *ghee* produced on her family farm. These were sometimes stuffed with tart pomegranate seeds and sometimes with cauliflower. We ate them with a sweet-and-sour, home-made turnip pickle.

Another friend was a Muslim from Uttar Pradesh, known to bring beef cooked with spinach, all deliciously flavoured with chillies, cardamom and cloves. Many of us were Hindus and not supposed to eat beef. So we just pretended not to know what it was. Our fingers would work busily around the tender meat that covered the bones and our cheeks would hollow as we sucked up the spicy marrow from the marrow bones. But we never asked what we were eating. The food was far too good for that. On the other hand, whenever my father went boar-hunting and we cooked that meat at home, I never took it to school. I knew it would offend my Muslim friends.

Another member of our gang was a Jain from Gujerat. Jains are vegetarians, some of them so orthodox as to refrain from eating beetroots and tomatoes because their colour reminds them of blood, and root vegetables because in pulling them out of the earth some innocent insect might have to lose its life. This friend occasionally brought the most delicious pancakes – *pooras* – made out of pulses.

One of us came from Kashmir, India's northernmost state. As she thrilled us with tales about tobogganing – the rest of us had never seen snow – she would unpack morel mushrooms from Kashmiri forests, cooked with tomatoes and peas and flavoured with asafetida. This friend was a Hindu, of course. Only Kashmiri Hindus cook with asafetida. And they do not cook with garlic. Kashmiri Muslims cook with garlic and frown upon asafetida. I found all this much easier to follow than algebra.

We had a South Indian friend too, a Syrian Christian from Kerala. She often brought *idlis*, slightly sour, steamed rice cakes that we ate with *sambar*, a pulse and fresh vegetable stew.

I, a Delhi Hindu, tried to dazzle my friends with quail and partridge which my father shot regularly and which our cook prepared with onions, ginger, cinnamon, black pepper and yoghurt.

India is such a large country – over a million square miles of changing topography, divided into thirty-one states and territories. Geography and local produce have played a great part in forming regional culinary traditions. Religious groups within each state have modified these regional cuisines even further to suit their own restrictions. History too, has had its influences. Goa, for example, on India's west coast, was ruled by the Portuguese for four centuries. Many of its people were converted to Catholicism, some by Saint Francis Xavier himself, and eventually developed an eating style that included platters of beef roulade – a stuffed roll of beef cooked in garlic-flavoured olive oil – and a dessert of layered pancakes – *bibingka* – made with egg yolks, coconut milk and raw Indian sugar. British colonialists left quite a few dishes in their wake too. There were those *cutlis* (cutlets) that our cook made. He, of course, marinated them in ginger and garlic first. Then, there was the strong influence of the Moguls. They had come to India via Persia in the sixteenth century and introduced the subcontinent to delicate *pullaos* and meats cooked with yoghurt and fried onions.

If there is a common denominator in all Indian foods, it is, perhaps, the imaginative use of spices. Does this mean that Indian food is always spicy? Well, in a sense it does. It always uses spices, sometimes just one spice to cook a potato dish and sometimes up to fifteen spices to make an elaborate meat dish. But it is not always hot. The 'heat' in Indian food comes from hot chillies. Chilli peppers were introduced to Asia in the sixteenth century by the Portuguese who had discovered them in the New World. Our own pungent spices until that time were the more moderate mustard seeds and black peppercorns. Those of you who do not like hot food should just leave out all the chillies – red, green or cayenne – in my recipes. Your food will still be authentically Indian, superb in flavour and not at all hot.

The spices and seasonings that we *do* like to use in our food include cumin, coriander, turmeric, black pepper, mustard seeds, fennel seeds, cinnamon, cardamom and cloves. Sometimes we leave the spices whole and fry them, sometimes we roast the spices and at other times we grind them and mix them with water or vinegar to make a paste. Each of these techniques draws out a completely different flavour from the same spice. This way we can give a great variety to, say, a vegetable like a potato, not only by methods such as boiling, baking and roasting but by cooking it with whole cumin one time, a combination of ground cumin and roasted fennel seeds another time and black pepper a third time. The permutations become endless as does the possibility of variety in tastes.

Does this mean that you cannot cook Indian food without having a whole lot of spices? I suggest that you start off by buying the specific spices you need to cook a selected dish and then slowly increase your spice 'wardrobe'. It is a bit like being a painter, I suppose. If you have a palette glowing with magenta and cobalt blue and sap green and vermilion, it will give you the confidence – and the choice – to do anything you want. You could use one colour, if you desired, or ten. It is the same with spices. It is nice to know that they are there. Whole spices last a long time. This way, you can cook aubergines with fennel seeds one day and green beans with cumin seeds the next day, if that is what you want.

Once you have mastered the use of Indian spices, you will find yourself not only cooking Indian meals but also inventing dishes with an Indian flavour and using Indian spices in unexpected ways. A French chef who once observed me cooking, now regularly uses ground roasted cumin seeds in his cream of tomato soup. I myself have created an Indian-style dish of pork chipolatas for this book to start you off in this pleasant direction. So don't be afraid to experiment – and have fun!

spices, seasonings and flavourings

Many of the spices used in Indian foods can be found in supermarkets. These include cumin, coriander, turmeric, cloves, cinnamon, cardamom, nutmeg, black pepper, bay leaves, ginger, paprika and cayenne pepper. Others have to be sought out from delicatessens and Greek, Indian or Pakistani grocers. Such grocers can be found in all major cities and in many small towns as well. It is also possible to order spices by post and on the Internet.

Ideally speaking, it is best to buy all dry spices in their whole form. They will stay fresh for long periods if stored in cool, dry, dark places in tightly lidded jars. This way you can grind the spices as you need them. I use an electric coffee-grinder for this purpose although a pestle and mortar would do. The more freshly ground the spices, the better their flavour. If you can only buy ground spices, buy small quantities and store them, too, in cool, dry, dark places in tightly lidded jars.

When transferring spices from plastic packets to jars, be sure to label them. When buying spices from ethnic grocers, make sure that they are labelled. Many of my cooking students have come to me with unlabelled jars and asked, 'What do I have here?' Even I, who have been cooking now for more than thirty years, cannot tell the difference between ground cumin and ground coriander without tasting or smelling them first.

Here is a list of the spices, seasonings and flavourings used in this book.

AMCHOOR Green Mango Powder

Unripe, sour, green mangoes are sliced and dried in the sun. Indian grocers sell both the dried slices and ground *amchoor*. Only the ground version is called for in this book. *Amchoor* is one of the many souring agents used in Indian cuisine. The powder can get lumpy so crush it well between your fingers before sprinkling it over foods.

ASAFETIDA Heeng

The Indian source for this smelly resin has traditionally been Afghanistan and western Kashmir. In its lump form, asafetida looks rather like the brown rosin my husband uses on the bow of his violin. Its smell is another matter. James Beard, America's foremost food writer, once compared the smell to that of fresh truffles. This seasoning is a digestive and is used in very small quantities. (It can even cure horses of indigestion!) A pinch of it is thrown into very hot oil and allowed to fry for a second before other foods are added. As asafetida is not widely available in supermarkets, I have made its use optional in most of my recipes. If you wish to purchase it, I suggest that you buy the smallest box available of *ground* asafetida. Make sure that the lid sits tightly on the box when you store it.

Clockwise from top left: Ground cardamom seed, cardamom pods and whole cardamom seed

CARDAMOM, PODS AND SEEDS Elaichi

Cardamom pods are whitish or green and have parchment-like skins and lots of round, black, highly aromatic seeds inside. The whitish pods are more readily available in supermarkets. They have been bleached and have less flavour and aroma than the unbleached green ones. For my recipes, use whichever pods you can find easily, although the green ones are better.

Many of my recipes call for whole pods. They are used as a flavouring in both savoury and sweet dishes. When used whole, cardamom pods are not meant to be eaten. We leave them on the side of the plate, along with any bones. When a recipe calls for cardamom *seeds*, you can either take the seeds out of the pods (a somewhat tedious task, best done while watching television) or else you can buy the seeds from the few Indian and Pakistani grocers who sell them. If my recipe calls for a small amount of *ground* cardamom seeds, pulverize them in a mortar.

CAYENNE PEPPER Pisi hui lal mirch

Made from dried red chillies, this is called red chilli powder by Indian and Pakistani grocers. Most of my recipes have a flexible amount of cayenne pepper in them. It is hard to know how hot people like their food. Use the smaller amount if you want your food just mildly hot and the larger amount if you want it hotter.

CHILLIES, FRESH, HOT, GREEN Hari mirch

These fresh chillies, 5–10 cm (2–4 inches) long, green outside and filled with flat round, white seeds, are rich in vitamins A and C. They give Indian foods a very special flavour.

Green chillies should be stored unwashed and wrapped in newspaper, in a plastic container in the refrigerator. Any chillies that go bad should be thrown away as they affect the whole batch.

Note: Be careful when handling cut green chillies. Refrain from touching your eyes or your mouth; wash your hands as soon as possible, otherwise you will 'burn' your skin with the irritant the chillies contain. If you want the green chilli flavour without most of the heat, remove the white seeds.

Above:
Cayenne pepper

CHILLIES, DRIED, HOT, RED Sabut lal mirch

These chillies, about 4–5 cm (1½–2 inches) long and 7 mm–1 cm (⅓–½ inches) wide, are often thrown into hot oil for a few seconds until they puff up and their skin darkens. This fried skin adds its own very special flavour to a host of meats, vegetables and pulses. Handle these chillies carefully, making sure that you wash your hands well before you touch your face. If you want the flavour of the chillies without their heat, make a small opening in them and then shake out and discard their seeds.

CINNAMON Dar cheeni

We often use cinnamon sticks whole in meat and rice dishes. They are used just for their flavour and aroma and are not meant to be eaten.

CLOVES, WHOLE Long

We often use whole cloves in our meat and rice dishes for their flavour and aroma. They are not meant to be eaten. (It must be added that we do suck on cloves as a mouth-freshener.)

COCONUT, FRESH GRATED Nariyal

When buying coconuts, make sure that they are crack-free and have no mould on them. Shake them to make sure that they are heavy with liquid. Now hold a coconut in one hand over a sink and hit it around the centre with the claw end of a hammer or with the blunt side of a heavy cleaver. The coconut should crack and break into two halves. (You could, if you like, collect the liquid in a cup. It is not used in cooking, but you may drink it. I do. I consider it my reward for breaking open the coconut in the first place.) Taste a piece of the coconut to make sure it is sweet and not rancid. Prise off the coconut flesh from the hard shell with a knife. If it proves to be too obstinate and you have a gas hob, it helps to put the coconut halves, cut side up, directly over a low flame, turning them around now and then so they char slightly. The woody shell contracts and releases the kernel.

Now peel off the brown coconut skin with a potato peeler and break the flesh into 2.5 cm (1 inch) pieces (larger ones if you are grating manually). Wash off these coconut pieces and either grate them finely on a hand grater or else put them in an electric blender or food processor. Do not worry about turning them into pulp in these electric machines. What you will end up with will be very finely 'grated' coconut, perfect for all the Indian dishes that require it. Grated coconut freezes beautifully and defrosts fast. I always grate large quantities whenever I have the time and store it in the freezer for future use.

COCONUT MILK

Coconut milk is made by grating coconut, mixing it with water and then squeezing out the juice. Since coconuts in the West vary so much in their freshness, I find it much easier to use a good brand of tinned coconut milk. I like Chaokoh, which is a Thai brand. The cream in coconut milk rises to the top of the can so follow the recipe directions regarding stirring or not stirring its contents.

CORIANDER, FRESH GREEN Hara dhaniya or kothmir

This is one of India's favourite herbs and is used, just as parsley might be, both as a garnish and for its flavour. This pretty green plant grows about 15–20 cm (6–8 inches) in height. Just the top, leafy section is used, though the stems are sometimes thrown into pulse dishes for their aroma.

To store fresh green coriander, put it in its unwashed state, roots and all, into a container filled with water, almost as if you were putting flowers in a vase. The leafy section of the plant should not be in water. Pull a polythene bag over the coriander and container and refrigerate. The fresh coriander should last for weeks. Every other day, pick off and discard yellowing leaves. Parsley can be used as a substitute.

CORIANDER SEEDS, WHOLE AND GROUND Dhania, sabut and pisa

These are the round, beige seeds of the coriander plant. They are used a lot in Indian cooking, generally in their ground form. You may buy them already ground, or you could buy the whole seeds and grind them yourself in small quantities in an electric coffee-grinder. I like to put my home-ground coriander seeds through a sieve though this is not essential.

Ground coriander seeds, if stored for several months, begin to taste a little like sawdust. It is best to discard them at this stage and start off with a fresh batch.

Clockwise from top: Fennel seeds, cumin seeds, fenugreek seeds (right) and mustard seeds (left)

CUMIN SEEDS, WHOLE AND GROUND Zeera, sabut and pisa

These caraway-like seeds are used very frequently in Indian food, both in their whole and ground forms. Whole seeds keep their flavour much longer than ground ones and may be ground very easily in an electric coffee-grinder.

ROASTED CUMIN SEEDS: Put 4–5 tablespoons of whole cumin seeds into a small, heavy frying-pan (cast-iron frying-pans are best for this) and place the pan over medium heat. No fat is necessary. Stir the seeds and keep roasting them until they turn a few shades darker. Soon you will be able to recognize the wonderful 'roasted' aroma that these seeds emit when they are ready. Store in an air-tight container.

GROUND, ROASTED CUMIN SEEDS: Empty the roasted seeds into an electric coffee-grinder or other spice-grinder and grind them finely. You could also use a pestle and mortar for this or else put the seeds between two sheets of brown paper and crush them with a rolling pin. Store ground, roasted cumin seeds in a tightly lidded jar.

CUMIN SEEDS, BLACK Shah zeera or kala zeera

These fine seeds are darker and more expensive than regular cumin seeds. They look like caraway seeds but have a gentle flavour. Buy them whole. If you cannot find them, use regular cumin seeds as a substitute.

FENNEL SEEDS Sonf

These seeds taste and look like anise seeds only they are larger, plumper and milder. They give meat and vegetables a delicious, liquorice-like flavour. Indians often serve roasted fennel seeds at the end of a meal as a digestive and mouth-freshener.

FENUGREEK SEEDS Methi

These yellow, squared-off seeds are used sparingly as they have a strong, earthy odour. They are used in pickling, curry powders and vegetarian dishes.

GARAM MASALA

This is an aromatic mixture that generally incorporates spices which are supposed to heat the body (the words mean 'hot spices') such as large black cardamoms, cinnamon, black cumin (also called *shah zeera* or *royal cumin*), cloves, black peppercorns and nutmeg. The mixture is used sparingly and is generally put into foods towards the end of their cooking period. It is also used as a garnish – a final aromatic flavouring sprinkled over cooked meats, vegetables and pulses.

Garam masala is not a standardized spice mixture. Apart from the fact that there are many regional variations, I am sure that every north Indian and Pakistani home has its own family recipe. The recipe here happens to be one of my favourites. I have substituted seeds from the green cardamom pods for the more traditional black ones as I find their taste to be far more delicate.

Indian and Pakistani grocers and most supermarkets do sell a ready-made *garam masala* which you may certainly resort to in emergencies. However, you will find it quite pallid, as cheaper spices such as cumin and coriander are often substituted for the more expensive cardamom and cloves.

It is best to grind *garam masala* in small quantities so that it stays fresh. My recipe makes about 3 tablespoons.

1 tablespoon cardamom seeds

5 cm (2 inch) cinnamon stick

1 teaspoon black cumin seeds (use regular cumin seeds as a substitute)

1 teaspoon cloves

1 teaspoon black peppercorns

$1/4$ average-sized nutmeg

Place all the ingredients in a clean, electric coffee-grinder (or any other spice-grinder). Turn the machine on for 30–40 seconds or until the spices are finely ground. Store in a small jar with a tight-fitting lid.

Remember to keep it away from heat and sunlight.

SESAME SEEDS Til

I use the beige, unhulled seeds that are sold in all health food stores and all oriental grocers. They have a wonderful, nutty flavour, especially after they have been roasted.

TURMERIC Haldi

This is the spice that makes many Indian foods yellow. Apart from its mild, earthy flavour, it is used mainly because it is a digestive and an antiseptic. Fresh turmeric looks like the baby sister of fresh ginger. They are both rhizomes. Buy the ground kind. Use it carefully as it can stain.

VARK

This airy, real-silver tissue is used for garnishing sweets as well as festive meat and rice dishes. It is sold only at some Indian and Pakistani grocers. Each silver tissue is packed between sheets of paper. Remove the top sheet carefully. Then pick up the next sheet with the *vark* on it and overturn it gently on the food you wish to garnish. Try not to let the *vark* disintegrate. It is edible. Store it in a tightly closed tin as it can tarnish.

VEGETABLE OIL

Most of my recipes call, rather generally, for vegetable oil. You could use what is labelled as vegetable oil in the supermarkets or you could use groundnut oil, corn oil, sunflower oil or simple olive oil. All would be quite suitable.

YELLOW AND RED FOOD COLOURINGS

These are used on some Indian foods — for instance these give *tandoori* food its distinctive colouring. They are vegetable colourings and have no taste. However, one word of warning: a few people (and that includes me!) are allergic to the tartrazine contained in these colourings.

Opposite: Turmeric

equipment

If you are going to cook authentic Indian food, do you need any special kitchen equipment? For those of you who already have well-equipped kitchens, the answer is probably 'no'. Good knives, sturdy pans with a good distribution of heat, rolling pins, graters, bowls, slotted spoons, pestle and mortar, frying-pans – I am sure you have these already. There are, however, a few items that make the cooking of Indian food simpler.

AN ELECTRIC FOOD PROCESSOR OR BLENDER Every Indian home has a grinding stone. This consists of a large, flat stone that just sits and a smaller stone that is moved manually on top of it and does the grinding. These stones are exceedingly heavy. It is just as well that they are no longer essential. Their place, in modern kitchens, can be taken by food processors and blenders. Onions, garlic and ginger, formerly ground on grinding stones, can now be made into a paste in electrically powered machines.

If you do not have a food processor or blender, then there are ways around it. Garlic, for example, may be mashed in a mortar or put through a garlic press. Ginger may be grated on the finest part of the grater. Onions can just be chopped very finely. Sometimes my recipe suggests putting water into the food processor while making the paste. If you have crushed the garlic and grated the ginger by hand, just put them into a bowl and add the amount of water in the recipe.

If you decide to go out and buy a blender, make sure that its blades sit close to the bottom, otherwise it will not pulverize small quantities adequately.

MICROPLANE GRATER This is the best gadget I have found for grating fresh, peeled ginger to a pulp.

AN ELECTRIC COFFEE-GRINDER Food processors and blenders cannot do all the work of an Indian grinding stone. Dry spices, for example, cannot be ground in them properly. For this, only a coffee-grinder will do. A coffee-grinder grinds spices in seconds and can then be wiped clean. If you do not have one, you will have to crush your spices in small quantities with a pestle and mortar.

TONGS My favourite tongs are intended for barbecues but I use them for turning chicken pieces, picking up meat pieces when they are browning, and even for tossing a salad.

A LARGE NON-STICK FRYING-PAN WITH A LID Non-stick pans really take the worry out of cooking many foods. Browning meats do not stick to the bottom, nor do sauces with ginger or almonds. As metal spoons ruin the finish of non-stick utensils, it is best to have a set of plastic or wooden ones.

SMALL AND LARGE CAST-IRON FRYING-PANS I keep a 13 cm (5 inch) cast-iron frying-pan for roasting spices – it can heat without oil or water in it – and for doing *baghaar*, frying small amounts of spices in oil. A larger cast-iron pan is excellent for making Indian breads such as *parathas* and *chapatis*. In India, these breads are cooked on a *tava*, a round, concave cast-iron plate. A large cast-iron frying-pan makes the best substitute.

KARHAI This is very similar to a Chinese wok. If you took a large, hollow ball and cut it into half, that would be about the shape of a *karhai*. I am not suggesting that you go out and buy a *karhai*. I just wish to point out that for deep-frying it is perhaps the most economical utensil, as it allows you to use a relatively small quantity of oil while giving you enough depth in the centre of the utensil to submerge foods. A deep frying-pan can be substituted for a *karhai*.

ELECTRIC RICE COOKERS If you frequently cook large quantities of rice, an electric rice cooker can be a useful piece of equipment. The cooker has a large covered pan which sits on top of an electric element. When the water has been absorbed by the rice the cooker switches itself off, and will then keep the rice warm for several hours. The preparation of the rice and the amount of water you use are identical to the conventional methods of cooking rice.

techniques

Indian food is unique in its imaginative use of spices, seasonings and flavourings. Many of our cooking techniques are really ways of getting these same spices, seasonings and flavourings to yield as great a variety of tastes and textures as possible. Spices and herbs do not have single, limited tastes. Depending upon how they are used – whole, ground, roasted, fried – they can be coaxed into producing a much larger spectrum than you might first imagine. Herein lies the genius of Indian cooking.

It amuses me to find that many of the techniques used in nouvelle cuisine have been used in India for centuries. We are told that sauces can be made much lighter if they are thickened with ingredients other than flour. Flour is almost never used as a thickener for Indian sauces. Instead, we have used, very cleverly, I might add, ingredients such as onions, garlic, ginger, yoghurt and tomatoes.

I think it might be useful, before you actually start cooking a recipe from this book, to measure and prepare all the ingredients you need for the recipe and have them ready near the cooker. Once you are experienced, this will not matter as much. But for those of you who are new to Indian cookery, it will help if you make all your pastes and do all your chopping and measuring before you start. The reason for this is that many Indian dishes require you to cook in one, flowing sweep. Ingredient follows ingredient, often swiftly. Frequently there is no time to stop and hunt for a spice that is hidden in the back of a cupboard. Something on the cooker might burn if you do. So organize yourself and read the recipe carefully. If many of the ingredients go into the pan at the same time, you can measure them out and keep them in the same bowl or plate.

Here are some of the more commonly used techniques.

CLARIFYING BUTTER Ghee: Not all Indian food is cooked in *ghee*, as some people imagine. Many of our foods are *meant* to be cooked in vegetable oil. But *ghee* does have a rich, nutty taste and a spoonful of it is frequently put on top of cooked pulses to enrich them and give them a silky smoothness. I must add here that there are certain families in India (not ours) who have always cooked in *ghee*. There used to be a certain amount of status attached to being able to say, 'We use nothing but pure *ghee*'. But today, even these families are coming around to using unsaturated fats.

I feel that cooking in *ghee* is a bit like cooking in butter. It is fine to do it some of the time for certain selected dishes. Some of my recipes do call for *ghee*. I suggest you buy it, ready-made, from Asian grocers. However, if you wish to make it yourself, melt 450 g (1 lb) unsalted butter in a small, heavy pan over low heat. Then let it simmer very gently for 10–30 minutes. The length of the time will depend upon the amount of water in the butter. As soon as the white, milky residue turns to golden particles (you have to keep watching), strain the *ghee* through several layers of cheesecloth or a large handkerchief. Cool and then pour into a clean jar. Cover. Properly made *ghee* does not need refrigeration.

DROPPING SPICES INTO HOT OIL Baghaar: I do not know of this technique being used anywhere else in the world. Oil (or *ghee*) is heated until it is extremely hot, but not burning. Then spices, generally whole ones, or else chopped up garlic and ginger, are added to the oil. The seasonings immediately begin to swell, brown, pop or otherwise change character. This seasoned oil, together with all the spices in it, is then poured over cooked foods such as pulses and vegetables or else uncooked foods are added to it and then sautéed or simmered. The seasonings that are most commonly used for *baghaar* include cumin seeds, black mustard seeds, fennel seeds, dried red chillies, cloves, cinnamon sticks, cardamom pods, bay leaves and black peppercorns as well as chopped up garlic and ginger. Hot oil transforms them all and gives them a new, more concentrated character. When the whole spices used are large, such as bay leaves, cinnamon sticks or even cloves and peppercorns, they are not meant to be eaten but are left to one side of the plate.

Above:
Spices dropped
into hot oil

GRINDING SPICES Many recipes call for ground spices. In India, we generally buy our spices whole and then grind them ourselves as and when we need them. They have much more flavour this way. You probably already know the difference between freshly ground black pepper and ground pepper that has been sitting around for a month. The same applies to all spices. In India, the grinding of spices is generally done on heavy grinding stones. We, in our modern kitchens, can get the same results without the labour by using an electric coffee-grinder. It is best to grind limited quantities so that the spices do not lose their flavour. If you wipe the grinder carefully after use there will be no 'aftertaste' of spices to flavour your coffee beans.

Buying ground spices is perfectly all right as long as you know that they will be less potent as time goes on. Before buying your spices, consult the preceding chapter to see which spices you must buy whole and which you may buy ground.

ROASTING SPICES This brings out yet another flavour from the spices. In my home, for example, we always make yoghurt relishes with cumin that has been roasted first and then ground. Nothing else will do. Ordinary ground cumin has a different flavour, quite unsuitable for putting into foods that are not going to be cooked. This roasting is best done in a heavy, cast-iron frying-pan since the pan can be heated without putting oil or water into it first. Whole spices are put into the pan. The pan is then shaken around until the spices turn a shade or two darker and emit their new 'roasted' aroma. You will begin to recognize it after you have done it a few times.

MAKING THICK SAUCES Many of our meat, poultry and fish dishes have thick, dark sauces. My mother always said that the mark of a good chef was his sauce, which depended not only on a correct balance of all the ingredients, but also on the correct frying (*bhuno*-ing) of these ingredients.

As I stated earlier, there is no flour in these sauces. The 'body' comes, very often, from onions, garlic and ginger. The rich brown colour comes from frying all these ingredients properly. Very often, we make a paste of one or more of these ingredients first. In India, this is done on a grinding stone but in Western kitchens it can be done easily in food processors and blenders, sometimes with the aid of a little water.

Once the paste has been made, it needs to be browned or the sauce will not have the correct flavour and colour. This is best done in a heavy pan, preferably non-stick, in a *generous* amount of oil. Remember that extra oil can always be spooned off the top once the dish has been cooked.

BROWNING SLICED OR CHOPPED ONIONS AND GARLIC Sometimes a recipe requires that you brown thinly sliced or chopped onions. I have noticed that many of the students in my cookery classes stop half-way and when I point out to them that the onions are not quite done, they say 'Oh, but if we cook them more, they will burn'. They will not, not if you watch. Start the frying on medium-high heat and turn the heat down somewhat as the onions lose their water and begin to turn brown. They do need to be a rich reddish-brown colour or your sauce – if that is what they are intended for – will be pale and weak.

The same goes for garlic. There is a common misconception that if garlic is allowed to pick up any colour at all, it will turn bitter. Actually, garlic tastes quite superb if it is chopped and allowed to fry in oil until it turns a medium-brown colour. I often cook courgettes this way – in oil that has been flavoured with browned garlic. Spinach and cauliflower taste good this way too. In India, we say that such dishes are cooked with a garlic *baghaar*. A garlic *baghaar* can, of course, just be the first step in a recipe. More spices would be added later.

ADDING YOGHURT TO SAUCES Yoghurt adds a creamy texture and a delicate tartness to many of our sauces. But yoghurt curdles when it is heated. So when we add it to our browning sauces, we add just 1 tablespoon at a time. After a tablespoon of yoghurt has been put in, it is stirred and fried until it is absorbed and 'accepted' by the sauce. Then the next tablespoon is added.

PEELING AND CHOPPING TOMATOES Many of my recipes call for peeled and chopped tomatoes. To peel them, bring a pan of water to a rolling boil. Drop in the tomatoes for 15 seconds. Drain, rinse under cold water and peel. Now chop the tomatoes, making sure that you save all the juice that comes out of them. In India, we very rarely seed tomatoes. Many people do not even bother to peel them though I do feel that this improves the texture of a sauce.

REDUCING SAUCES Sometimes meat is allowed to cook in a fairly thin, brothy sauce. Then the lid of the pan is removed and the sauce reduced over fairly high heat until it is thick and clings to the meat. The meat has to be stirred frequently at this stage, so that it does not catch and burn.

COOKING CHICKEN WITHOUT ITS SKIN In India, we almost always remove the skin of the chicken before we cook it. The flavour of the spices penetrates the chicken much better this way and the entire dish is less fatty. It is very easy to remove the skin. Just hold it with kitchen paper so that it does not slip, and pull!

MARINATING We often cut deep gashes in large pieces of meat and leave them overnight in a marinade of yoghurt and seasonings. The yoghurt tenderizes the meat while the gashes allow the flavour to penetrate deep inside the meat. After this, the meat can be grilled or baked faster than usual.

BROWNING MEATS In India, we generally do not brown cubes of meat by themselves but brown them with the sauce instead. However, in the West many meats release far too much water as they cook – Indian meats tend to be very fresh and have far less water in them. So to avoid this problem I brown my meat a few pieces at a time in hot oil and set them aside. Once I have made the sauce, I add the browned meat cubes (and all the good juices that come out of them) and let them cook.

These are just a few of the techniques that we use in Indian cookery. Others, that have to do with cooking rice or pulses, are dealt with in the relevant chapters.

Above:
Marinating chicken

menus

AND HOW TO EAT INDIAN FOOD

What do you eat with what? I have suggested accompaniments for the recipes in this book. You do not have to follow my suggestions. After all, the fun of eating is to follow your own palate and put together dishes that are convenient and exciting for you.

Generally speaking, an Indian meal consists of a meat dish, a vegetable dish, bread and/or rice, a pulse dish, a yoghurt relish (or plain yoghurt) and a fresh chutney or small, relish-like salad. Pickles and preserved chutneys may be added if you have them. Fruit rather than desserts is served at the end of a meal, although on festive occasions sweets would not be at all amiss. Sometimes, when the meat dish is particularly elegant and rich, we eliminate the pulse and serve an equally elegant *pullao* rice. Vegetarians – of whom there are millions in India – increase the number of vegetable and pulse dishes and always serve yoghurt in some form.

Within this general framework, we try to see that the dishes we serve vary in colour, texture and flavour. If the meat, for example, has a lot of sauce, then we often serve a 'dry', unsauced vegetable with it. If the vegetable we are serving is very soft – such as spinach – we make sure that there is a crunchy relish around on the table.

Most Indians like to eat with their hands. The more Westernized ones may use knives and forks or spoons and forks, or just forks, but they too succumb every now and then to the pleasure of eating with their fingers.

It is only the right hand that is used for eating, the left being considered 'unclean'. With it, we break pieces of bread and then use the pieces to scoop up some meat or vegetable. With it, we also form neat

morsels out of rice and other accompanying dishes and then transport them to our mouths. In the northern states such as Uttar Pradesh, this is done very delicately with just the tips of the fingers. In the south, almost the entire hand may be used. Needless to say, hands must be washed before and after eating. Even the humblest of roadside stalls catering to simple villagers and truck drivers would not consider offering food before offering a *lota* (water vessel) of water for washing first.

When we serve ourselves, we put most foods beside each other on our plates. Only very wet, flowing dishes are sometimes ladled on top of the rice but not on top of *all* the rice. Some of the rice is left plain to enable us to eat it with other dishes. Very wet dishes that are meant to be eaten with bread are served in small, individual bowls.

This is all very well if you are cooking a whole Indian meal. If you feel like making such a meal, then by all means, do it. On the other hand, there is no reason why you cannot serve an Indian vegetable with your roast lamb or eat an Indian meat (such as Chicken in a Butter Sauce, page 92) with French bread and a salad. If you are on a diet, you could make yourself a Yoghurt with Cucumber and Mint (page 210) for lunch and follow it with a crunchy apple. I have even served a roast leg of lamb with Black-eyed Beans with Mushrooms (page 174), Simple Buttery Rice with Onion (page 194), and a green salad. It is an easy meal to put together *and* it is good.

suggested menus

Here are some suggestions for a variety of delicious meals for everyday eating or entertaining.

Serves 6

Mughlai Lamb with Turnips, *Shabdeg* (page 75)

Mushroom Pullao, *Khumbi pullao* (page 199)

Spicy Green Beans, *Masaledar sem* (page 132)

Yoghurt with Cucumber and Mint, *Kheere ka raita* (page 210)

Serves 4

Prawns in a Dark Sauce, *Rasedar jhinga* (page 119)

Plain Basmati Rice, *Basmati chaaval* (page 193)

Cauliflower with Potatoes, *Phool gobi aur aloo ki bhaji* (page 144)

Tomato, Onion and Green Coriander Relish, *Cachumber* (page 215)

Serves 6

Black-eyed Beans with Mushrooms, *Lobhia aur khumbi* (page 174)

Cauliflower with Onion and Tomato, *Phool gobi ki bhaji* (page 142)

Layered Bread, *Paratha* (page 179)

Gujerati Carrot Salad, *Gajar ka salad* (page 217)

Serves 4–6

Beef Baked with Yoghurt and Black Pepper, *Dum gosht* (page 69)

Aubergine Cooked in the Pickling Style, *Baigan achari* (page 136)

Rice and Peas, *Tahiri* (page 196)

Tomato, Onion and Green Coriander Relish, *Cachumber* (page 215)

Serves 4

Cod Steaks in a Spicy Tomato Sauce, *Timatar wali macchi* (page 122)

South Indian-style Light, Fluffy Rice, *Dakshini chaaval* (page 193)

Spicy Cucumber Wedges, *Kheere ke tukray* (page 218)

Serves 6

Shahjahani Leg of Lamb, *Shahjahani raan* (page 78)

Aromatic Yellow Rice, *Peelay chaaval* (page 200)

Green Beans with Ginger and Green Coriander, *Hare masale ki sem* (page 133)

Drunken Orange Slices, *Sharabi narangi* (page 225)

Serves 6

Turkey Kebabs, *Turkey ke kabab* (page 104)

Potatoes with Black Pepper, *Bengali aloo* (page 153)

Cabbage with Peas, *Bund gobi aur matar* (page 140)

Naan (page 184) or store-bought pitta bread

Serves 4

Chicken with Roasted Coriander in a Coconut Curry Sauce, *Dakshini murgh* (page 102)

Fried Aubergine Slices, *Tala hua baigan* (page 134)

Spiced Basmati Rice, *Masaledar basmati* (page 194)

Semolina Halva, *Sooji ka halva* (page 226)

Serves 6

Mughlai Chicken with Almonds and Sultanas, *Shahjahani murghi* (page 96)

Plain Basmati Rice, *Basmati chaaval* (page 193)

Moong Dal and Red Lentils with Browned Onions, *Mili moong aur masoor dal* (page 170)

'Dry' Okra, *Sookhi bhindi* (page 152)

Serves 4

Salmon Steamed with Crushed Mustard Seeds and Tomato, *Salmon bhapey* (page 124)

Simple Buttery Rice with Onion, *Pyaz wali basmati chaaval* (page 194)

Whole Green Lentils with Spinach and Ginger (page 168)

Mixed Vegetables in a Mustard and Cumin Sauce, *Shorvedar subzi* (page 158)

Indians love to munch. Whether they are on buses or trains, in cinemas or in parks, they can be spotted opening up newspaper cones, unwrapping tea-cloth bundles or easing eager hands into terracotta pots. Good things are hidden inside that can be nibbled upon for the satisfaction of the soul.

Take *samosas*, for instance, those triangular, savoury pastries. The best place to eat them is right on the street, when the odours wafting from a nearby *samosa*-maker become too overwhelming to resist. All kinds of kebabs, marinated and grilled meat cubes, are also sold at open stalls. This is done deliberately to entice passing strollers.

All workers in India stop for tea, a custom not too different from the British one. But what is served, is a bit different. There would be tea of course, perhaps *masala chai* ('spiced tea'; see page 234) or coffee. Then, an odd assortment might appear – *samosas*, fried cashews and, to sweeten the mouth, some carrot *halva* (see page 230)!

In this chapter, there are also snacks that may be served with drinks, such as cocktail *koftas* (meatballs) that lend themselves very well to having toothpicks stuck in them, and spicy potato matchsticks.

I have included some soups in this chapter as well. Even though we do not, as a nation, drink soups, most Westernized Indians have happily adapted soups from other nations to suit their own tastes.

soups, snacks and savouries

chicken mulligatawny soup

There are many soupy dishes in India that are served with rice. It was probably one of
these that inspired Anglo-Indian communities three centuries ago to create a soup
that had Indian spices and ingredients in it, yet could be served at the start of a meal.
There are hundreds of recipes for mulligatawny soup in India, all slightly different.
For this book, I have chosen one in which the base is a purée of red split lentils (*masoor
dal*). It is a hearty soup that can almost be a meal in itself. It is traditional to have
some plain boiled rice with this soup. I usually serve it on the side, in small quantities.

Serves 4 to 6

175 g (6 oz) red split lentils (*moong dal*),
picked over, washed and drained

1.2 litres (2 pints) chicken stock

½ teaspoon ground turmeric

100 g (4 oz) potatoes

5 cloves garlic, peeled

3 cm (1¼ inch) cube fresh ginger, peeled
and coarsely grated

4½ tablespoons plus 250 ml (8 fl oz) water

1 chicken breast, boned and skinned, with
a net weight of about 200 g (7 oz)

1¼ teaspoons salt

Freshly ground black pepper

3 tablespoons vegetable oil

1 teaspoon ground cumin

1 teaspoon ground coriander

⅛ –¼ teaspoon cayenne pepper

About 1 tablespoon lemon juice
(you might want more)

Combine the lentils, chicken stock and turmeric in a heavy, medium-sized pan
and bring to a boil. Cover, leaving the lid just very slightly ajar, turn heat to low,
and simmer gently for 30 minutes.

While the soup simmers, peel the potatoes and cut into 1 cm (½ inch) dice.
When the soup has cooked for 30 minutes, add the potato dice to it. Cover,
leaving the lid slightly ajar again, and continue the simmering for another
30 minutes.

During this second simmering period, put the garlic and ginger into the
container of an electric blender. Add 4½ tablespoons water and blend until you
have a smooth paste.

Remove all fat from the chicken breast and cut it into 1 cm (½ inch) dice. Put
the chicken in a bowl. Sprinkle ¼ teaspoon of the salt and some black pepper
over it. Toss to mix.

Once the soup base has finished cooking, it needs to be puréed. I do this in
a blender, in three batches. Put the puréed soup in a bowl. Add the remaining
1 teaspoon salt and mix.

Rinse and wipe out your soup pan. Pour the oil into it and set it over medium
heat. When the oil is hot, put in the garlic-ginger paste, the cumin, coriander and
cayenne. Fry, stirring continuously, until the spice mixture is slightly browned
and separates from the oil. Put in the chicken pieces. Stir and fry another 2–3
minutes or until the chicken pieces turn quite opaque. Add 250 ml (8 fl oz) water
and bring to a boil. Cover, turn heat to low and simmer for 3 minutes or until
chicken is cooked. Pour in the puréed soup and the lemon juice. Stir to mix and
bring to a simmer. Taste the soup for seasonings. I usually add another teaspoon
or so of lemon juice. Simmer the soup very gently for another 2 minutes. If it is
too thick, you can always thin it out with a little chicken stock or water.

green soup

Hara shorva

This is India's version of cream of pea soup. It is delicate and quite delicious.

Serves 5 to 6

900 g (4 oz) potatoes, peeled and
roughly diced

75 g (3 oz) onions, peeled and
coarsely chopped

1.2 litres (2 pints) chicken stock

2 cm (³/₄ inch) cube fresh ginger, peeled

¹/₂ teaspoon ground coriander

2 teaspoons ground cumin

5 tablespoons chopped, fresh
green coriander

¹/₂ fresh, hot green chilli

275 g (10 oz) shelled peas, fresh or frozen

³/₄ teaspoon salt (more if the
stock is unsalted)

1 tablespoon lemon juice

¹/₂ teaspoon ground, roasted cumin seeds
(page 20)

150 ml (5 fl oz) double cream

Combine the potatoes, onions, chicken stock, ginger, ground coriander and ground cumin in a pan and bring to a boil. Cover, turn heat to low and simmer for 30 minutes. Fish out the cube of ginger and discard it. Add the fresh coriander, green chilli, peas, salt, lemon juice and ground, roasted cumin seeds. Bring to a boil and simmer, uncovered, for 2–3 minutes or until the peas are just tender. Empty the soup into the container of an electric blender in 2 or 3 batches and blend until it is smooth. Put the soup into a clean pan. Add the cream and bring to a simmer to heat through.

delicious cocktail koftas

Chhote kofte

Almost every country has some type of meatball. This Indian one is made out of minced lamb and you can eat it as part of a meal or you could stick toothpicks into the *koftas* and serve them as snacks.

Makes 30 meatballs and serves 6 for snacks, 4 for dinner

FOR THE MEATBALLS

450 g (1 lb) minced lamb

$1/2$ teaspoon salt

1 teaspoon ground cumin

1 teaspoon ground coriander

$1/4$ teaspoon *garam masala* (page 21)

$1/8$ teaspoon cayenne pepper

2 tablespoons very finely chopped, fresh green coriander

3 tablespoons natural yoghurt

FOR THE SAUCE

5 cloves garlic, peeled

2.5 cm (1 inch) cube fresh ginger, peeled and coarsely chopped

4 tablespoons plus 300 ml (10 fl oz) water

1 teaspoon ground cumin

1 teaspoon ground coriander

1 teaspoon bright red paprika

$1/4$ teaspoon cayenne pepper

5 tablespoons vegetable oil

2.5 cm (1 inch) cinnamon stick

6 cardamom pods

6 cloves

100 g (4 oz) onions, peeled and finely chopped

100 g (4 oz) tomatoes, peeled (page 30) and chopped (a small can of tomatoes may be substituted)

4 tablespoons natural yoghurt

$1/2$ teaspoon salt

To make the meatballs: Combine all the ingredients for the meatballs. Dip your hands in water whenever you need to and form about 30 meatballs.

For the sauce, put the garlic and ginger into the container of a food processor or blender along with 4 tablespoons water. Blend until you have a paste. Put the paste in a bowl. Add the cumin, coriander, paprika and cayenne. Stir to mix.

To make the sauce: Put the oil in a heavy, 23–25 cm (9–10 inch) wide pan or frying-pan and set over medium-high heat. When hot, put in the cinnamon, cardamom pods and cloves. Stir them for 3–4 seconds. Now put in the onions and fry them, stirring all the time, until they are reddish-brown in colour. Turn the heat to medium and put in the paste from the bowl as well as the chopped tomatoes. Stir and fry this mixture until it turns a brownish colour. When it begins to catch, add 1 tablespoon of the yoghurt. Stir and fry some more until the yoghurt is incorporated into the sauce. Now add another tablespoon of yoghurt. Incorporate that into the sauce as well. Keep doing this until you have put in all the yoghurt. Now put in 300 ml (10 fl oz) water and the salt. Stir and bring to a simmer.

Put in all the meatballs in a single layer. Cover, leaving the lid very slightly ajar, turn heat to low and cook for 25 minutes. Stir very gently every 5 minutes or so, making sure not to break the meatballs. Towards the end of the cooking period, you should scrape the bottom of the pan just to make sure the sauce is not catching. If necessary, add a tablespoon or so of water. Remove the lid and turn the heat up to medium-low. Stir gently and cook until the meatballs have a browned look. All the sauce should now be clinging to the meatballs and there should be just a little fat left at the bottom of the pan.

When you are ready to eat, heat the *koftas* gently. Lift them out of the fat and shake off any whole spices that may be clinging to them. Stick a toothpick into each *kofta* if serving with drinks.

If you have these *koftas* for dinner, you could leave more of a sauce.

tandoori-style prawns

These marinated prawns are traditionally cooked in a *tandoor*. I cook them very quickly in a frying-pan. You may easily double the recipe, if you wish to serve these prawns as a main course. Just use a larger frying-pan.

Serves 4 as a snack

4 tablespoons natural yoghurt

2.5 cm (1 inch) cube fresh ginger, peeled and very finely grated

1 large clove garlic, peeled and mashed to a pulp

5 teaspoons lemon juice

$1/4$ teaspoon salt, or to taste

Freshly ground black pepper

$1^1/2$ teaspoons ground, roasted cumin seeds (page 20)

$1/4$ teaspoon *garam masala* (page 21)

2 teaspoons yellow liquid food colouring mixed with 1 teaspoon red liquid food colouring

225 g (8 oz) peeled good-quality frozen prawns, defrosted and patted dry

50 g (2 oz) unsalted butter

Put the yoghurt in a bowl. Beat lightly with a fork or a whisk until it is smooth and creamy. Add the ginger, garlic, lemon juice, salt, some black pepper, ground, roasted cumin seeds, *garam masala* and liquid food colouring. Stir to mix and set aside for 15 minutes. Push this liquid through a sieve into a second bowl. Add the prawns to the marinade and mix well. Set aside for 30 minutes. Remove the prawns with a slotted spoon, leaving all the marinade behind in the bowl.

Melt the butter in a 20–23 cm (8–9 inch) frying-pan over medium heat. When the butter has melted completely, turn heat to medium-high and immediately pour in the marinade. Stir and fry for a few minutes or until the butter separates and you have a thick bubbly sauce clinging to the bottom of the pan. Add the prawns and fold them in. Cook for a few minutes, stirring gently. Do not overcook the prawns.

Serve immediately.

deep-fried, stuffed savoury pastry

Samosa

Samosas make excellent appetizers. If you wish to use a minced meat stuffing, use the recipe for Minced Lamb with Mint (page 59). Boil away the liquid and drain the fat. Stuff each *samosa* with about 2½ tablespoons of the cooked mince. *Samosas* are delicious with Fresh Coriander Chutney (page 218). Here is my recipe for *samosas* with a potato stuffing.

Makes 16 samosas

FOR THE PASTRY

225 g (8 oz) plain flour

½ teaspoon salt

4 tablespoons vegetable oil plus a bit more

4 tablespoons water

FOR THE STUFFING

725 g (1 lb 10 oz) potatoes, boiled in their jackets and allowed to cool

4 tablespoons vegetable oil

1 medium-sized onion, peeled and finely chopped

175 g (6 oz) shelled peas, fresh or frozen (if frozen, defrost them first)

1 tablespoon peeled, finely grated fresh ginger

1 fresh, hot green chilli, finely chopped

3 tablespoons very finely chopped, fresh green coriander

About 3 tablespoons water

1½ teaspoons salt, or to taste

1 teaspoon ground coriander

1 teaspoon *garam masala* (page 21)

1 teaspoon ground, roasted cumin seeds (page 20)

¼ teaspoon cayenne pepper

2 tablespoons lemon juice

Vegetable oil for deep-frying

Sift the flour and salt into a bowl. Add the 4 tablespoons of vegetable oil and rub it in with your fingers until the mixture resembles coarse breadcrumbs. Slowly add about 4 tablespoons water – or a tiny bit more – and gather the dough into a stiff ball.

Empty the ball out on to a clean work surface. Knead the dough for about 10 minutes or until it is smooth. Make a ball. Rub the ball with about ¼ teaspoon oil and slip it into a polythene bag. Set it aside for 30 minutes or longer.

Make the stuffing: Peel the potatoes and cut them into 5 mm (¼ inch) dice. Put 4 tablespoons oil in a large frying-pan and set over medium heat. When hot, put in the onions. Stir and fry them until they begin to turn brown at the edges. Add the peas, ginger, green chilli, fresh coriander and 3 tablespoons water. Cover, lower heat and simmer until the peas are cooked. Stir every now and then and add a little more water if the frying-pan seems to dry out.

Add the diced potatoes, salt, ground coriander, *garam masala*, ground, roasted cumin seeds, cayenne and lemon juice. Stir to mix. Cook on low heat for 3–4 minutes, stirring gently as you do so. Check balance of salt and lemon juice. You may want more of both. Turn off the heat and allow the mixture to cool.

Knead the pastry dough again and divide it into 8 balls. Keep 7 covered while you work with the eighth. Roll this ball out into a 18 cm (7 inch) round. Cut it into half with a sharp, pointed knife. Pick up one half and form a cone, making a 5 mm (¼ inch) wide overlapping seam. Glue this seam together with a little water. Fill the cone with about 2½ tablespoons of the potato mixture. Close the top of the cone by sticking the open edges together with a little water.

Again, your seam should be about 5 mm (¼ inch) wide. Press the top seam down with the prongs of a fork or flute it with your fingers. Make 15 more *samosas*.

Put about 4–5 cm (1½–2 inches) oil in a small, deep frying-pan or Indian *karhai* and set over medium-low heat. When the oil is medium-hot, put in as many *samosas* as the pan will hold in single layer. Fry slowly, turning the *samosas* frequently until they are golden-brown and crisp. Drain on kitchen paper and serve hot, warm or at room temperature.

his chapter has a great variety of meat dishes in it, going from *Kheema matar* (Minced Meat with Peas) and *Chhole wala gosht* (Pork Chops with Chick Peas) that you may wish to cook for your family, to *Raan masaledar* – a whole leg of lamb garnished with almonds and raisins – which would impress the most blasé of guests.

There are a lot of lamb recipes. We do eat a fair amount of lamb in India. We also eat a lot of goat. As goat is hard to find in the West, I have substituted lamb in its place. I find that the best cuts of lamb for stewing come from the neck and shoulder. You should buy a whole shoulder and carve up the meat yourself. Or you could buy shoulder chops and cut them up with a heavy cleaver. There is a lot of connective tissue in the shoulder and neck. This eventually makes for a moister meat.

In India, we usually leave the bone in the meat when we are cooking any stew-type dish. In fact, we throw in a few extra marrow bones for good measure because they affect the taste and texture of the sauce. However, many recipes in this book call for boned lamb. This is only because, over the years, I have seen many guests struggle with bones and have come to the conclusion that just because I like bones (I suck them), there is no reason to inflict them upon my guests. A majority of people who dine in our house seem to prefer boned meat. I leave the bone-in or bone-out decision up to you. Just remember that bones in stewing meat such as shoulder make up about 40 per cent of the total volume. If my recipe is for boned meat and you decide to leave the bone in, you might feed just half the number of people.

In India, we frequently cook meat with vegetables such as potatoes and turnips. They absorb its taste and lend their own flavour to the sauce.

I have included a few recipes for beef and pork as many communities in India eat them. I, for one, simply love the Beef Baked with Yoghurt and Black Pepper as well as the spicy and sour pork *vindaloo*, a Goan speciality.

meat

minced lamb with mint

Pudine wala kheema

This dish may be served with rice, a pulse (such as Whole Green Lentils with Spinach and Ginger, page 168) and a yoghurt relish. I often use it to stuff tomatoes. Get firm, good-sized tomatoes and slice off a cap at the top. Scoop out the inside without breaking the skin and then season the inside of the tomato with salt and pepper. Stuff loosely with the mince, put the caps back on and bake in a 200°C/400°F/Gas 6 oven for 15 minutes or until the skin begins to crinkle. Serve with rice and a salad.

Serves 6

175 g (6 oz) onions, peeled

8–9 cloves garlic, peeled

5 x 2.5 cm (2 x 1 inch) piece fresh ginger, peeled and coarsely chopped

3 tablespoons water

2 tablespoons ground cumin

4 teaspoons ground coriander

1 teaspoon ground turmeric

$1/4$ –1 teaspoon cayenne pepper

4 tablespoons vegetable oil

4 cardamom pods

6 cloves

900 g (2 lb) minced lamb

About $1^1/_4$ teaspoons salt

50 g (2 oz) finely chopped, fresh mint

$1/4$ teaspoon *garam masala* (page 21)

$1^1/_2$ tablespoons lemon juice

Chop half the onions finely and set aside. Chop the other half coarsely and put them, along with the garlic, ginger and water into the container of an electric blender. Blend to a smooth paste. Empty into a small bowl. Add the cumin, coriander, turmeric and cayenne. Mix.

Put the oil in a 25 cm (10 inch) frying-pan and set over high heat. When hot, put in the cardamom pods and cloves. Two seconds later, put in the finely chopped onions. Stir and fry them until they turn fairly brown. Turn the heat to medium and put in the spice mixture. Stir and fry for 3–4 minutes. If the spice mixture sticks to the pan, sprinkle in a tablespoon of water and keep frying.

Put in the minced meat. Break up all the lumps and stir the mince about until it loses all its pinkness. Stir and fry another minute after that. Add the salt and mix. Cover, turn heat to very low and let the mince cook in its own juices for 25 minutes. Remove the cover and spoon off most of the accumulated fat. Add the chopped mint, *garam masala* and lemon juice. Stir to mix and bring to a simmer. Cover, and simmer on very low heat for 3 minutes.

Note: The cardamom pods and cloves are not meant to be eaten.

kashmiri meatballs

Kashmiri koftas

These sausage-shaped 'meatballs' taste very Kashmiri in their final blend of flavours.
I often serve them with Plain Basmati Rice (page 193), Red Split Lentils with Cumin
Seeds (page 165), and Carrot and Onion Salad (page 217).

Serves 6

900 g (2 lb) minced lamb

Piece of fresh ginger, about 4 cm
(1½ inches) long and 2.5 cm
(1 inch) thick, peeled and finely grated

1 tablespoon ground cumin

1 tablespoon ground coriander

¼ teaspoon ground cloves

¼ teaspoon ground cinnamon

⅛ teaspoon grated nutmeg

¼ teaspoon freshly ground black pepper

⅛–¼ teaspoon cayenne pepper

About 1¼ teaspoons salt

5 tablespoons natural yoghurt

7–8 tablespoons vegetable oil

5 cm (2 inch) cinnamon stick

5–6 cardamom pods

2 bay leaves

5–6 cloves

250 ml (8 fl oz) warm water

Combine the lamb, ginger, cumin, coriander, ground cloves, ground cinnamon, grated nutmeg, black pepper, cayenne, salt and 3 tablespoons of the yoghurt in a bowl. Mix well.

Wet your hands with cold water and form 24 long *koftas* – sausage shapes, about 6–7.5 cm (2½–3 inches) long and about 2.5 cm (1 inch) thick.

Heat the oil in a large, preferably non-stick, frying-pan (or use two frying-pans). When hot, put in the cinnamon stick, cardamom pods, bay leaves and cloves. Stir for a second. Now put in the *koftas* in a single layer and fry them on medium-high heat until they are lightly browned on all sides. Beat the remaining yoghurt into the 250 ml (8 fl oz) warm water. Pour this over the *koftas* and bring to a boil. Cover, lower heat and simmer for about 30 minutes, turning the *koftas* around gently every 7–8 minutes. By the end of the 30 minutes no liquid other than the fat should be left in the frying-pan. If necessary, turn up the heat to achieve this.

When you get ready to serve, lift the *koftas* out of the fat with a slotted spoon. Leave the whole spices behind as well – they are not meant to be eaten.

lamb with spinach

Dilli ka saag gosht

This dish could also be made with beef. Use cubed chuck steak and cook it for about
2 hours or until it is tender. *Dilli ka saag gosht* may be served with rice or bread. I think
Fried Aubergine Slices (page 134) and a yoghurt dish would complement the meat well.

Serves 6

8 tablespoons vegetable oil

¹/₄ teaspoon black peppercorns

6–7 cloves

2 bay leaves

6 cardamom pods

175 g (6 oz) onions, peeled and
finely chopped

6–8 cloves garlic, peeled and
finely chopped

2.5 cm (1 inch) cube fresh ginger, peeled
and finely chopped

900 g (2 lb) boned lamb from the shoulder,
cut into 2.5 cm (1 inch) cubes

2 teaspoons ground cumin

1 teaspoon ground coriander

¹/₄ –³/₄ teaspoon cayenne pepper

2 teaspoons salt

5 tablespoons natural yoghurt,
well beaten

900 g (2 lb) fresh spinach, trimmed,
washed and finely chopped;
900 g (2 lb) frozen spinach, thawed out,
may be substituted

¹/₄ teaspoon *garam masala* (page 21)

Put the oil in a large pan and set over medium-high heat. When hot, put in the
peppercorns, cloves, bay leaves and cardamom pods. Stir for a second. Now put
in the onions, garlic and ginger. Stir and fry until the onions develop brown
specks. Now add the meat, cumin, coriander, cayenne and 1 teaspoon of the
salt. Stir and fry for a minute. Add 1 tablespoon of the beaten yoghurt. Stir and
fry for another minute. Add another tablespoon of the yoghurt. Stir and fry for
a minute. Keep doing this until all the yoghurt has been incorporated. The meat
should also have a slightly browned look. Add the spinach and the remaining
1 teaspoon salt. Stir to mix. Keep stirring and cooking until the spinach wilts
completely. Cover tightly and simmer on low heat for about 1 hour 10 minutes
or until the meat is tender.

Remove the lid and add the *garam masala*. Turn the heat to medium. Stir and
cook another 5 minutes or until most (but not all) the water in the spinach
disappears and you have a thick, green sauce.

Note: The whole spices in this dish are not meant to be eaten.

calves' liver in a gingery sauce

Kaleji

You may make this with calves' liver or, if you like, with lambs' or goats' liver. You could, of course, serve it as part of an Indian meal. However, if you are looking for a quick lunch or dinner idea or for something for an after-the-theatre supper, serve this on toast with a green salad on the side. You should cut the crusty edges off the slice of bread before toasting it. If you do not mind the calories, shallow-frying the bread in oil to make a large croûton makes the liver taste even better! The sauce can be made ahead of time. It is best to brown the liver and fold it into the sauce just before you eat.

Serves 3 to 4

5 cloves garlic, peeled and coarsely chopped

5 cm (2 inch) piece fresh ginger, peeled and coarsely chopped

1–2 fresh, hot green chillies, coarsely sliced

4 tablespoons plus 175 ml (6 fl oz) water

5 tablespoons vegetable oil

1/2 teaspoon cumin seeds

1/4 teaspoon *kalonji*

120 g (4 1/2 oz) onions, peeled and very finely chopped

6 tablespoons natural yoghurt

175 g (6 oz) tomatoes, finely chopped

Salt

1/2 teaspoon *garam masala* (page 21)

1/8 teaspoon cayenne pepper

450 g (1 lb) calves' liver, cut into 1 cm (1/2 inch) thick slices

Freshly ground black pepper

2 tablespoons finely chopped, fresh green coriander (optional)

Put the garlic, ginger, green chillies and 4 tablespoons water into the container of an electric blender or food processor. Blend until you have a paste.

Put 4 tablespoons of the oil in a large frying-pan and set over high heat. When hot, put in the cumin seeds and *kalonji*. Ten seconds later, put in the onions. Stir and fry until the onions turn a reddish-brown. Add the paste from the blender. Stir and fry it for 2–3 minutes. Put in 1 tablespoon of the yoghurt. Stir and cook until the yoghurt is incorporated into the sauce. Put in a second tablespoon of yoghurt and incorporate it into the sauce in the same way. Do this with all the yoghurt. Now put in the tomatoes. Stir and cook for a minute. Turn heat down to medium. Stir and cook for another 5 minutes. Add 3/4 teaspoon salt and the *garam masala* and cayenne. Stir and cook for another 2 minutes. Add about 175 ml (6 fl oz) water and bring to a simmer. Turn off heat. This is the sauce. Leave it in the frying-pan.

Shortly before eating, pat the liver pieces dry with kitchen paper. Sprinkle a little salt and lots of black pepper on both sides of the slices of liver. Put the remaining 1 tablespoon oil into a clean, preferably non-stick, frying-pan and set over high heat. When very hot, put in the slices of liver in a single layer. As soon as one side has browned, turn the slices over and brown the second side. Do not let the liver cook through and get hard. Remove the liver to a board and cut it into 1 cm (1/2 inch) cubes. Set the sauce over medium heat. When hot, put in the liver pieces and the fresh coriander if you are using it. Simmer for 1 minute, stirring once or twice. Serve.

beef baked with yoghurt and black pepper

Dum gosht

Ever since the Moguls came to India, there has been a method of cooking that Indians refer to as '*dum*'. Meat (or rice for that matter) is partially cooked in a heavy pot and then covered over with a flat lid. At this stage the pot and lid are sealed with a 'rope' made out of very stiff dough. The pot is placed over a gentle fire – generally the last of the charcoals – and more hot charcoals are spread over the lid. The meat proceeds to cook very slowly until it is tender, often in small amounts of liquid (the equivalent of slow oven baking today). So what I have done here is to update a very traditional Mogul recipe, modernizing it to suit our contemporary kitchens. *Dum* dishes do not have a lot of sauce. Ideally, whatever sauce there is should be thick and cling to the meat.

If you like, you could leave out the cayenne in this recipe. That is probably what the early Moguls did. The later Moguls, seduced by the chilli peppers brought over from the New World by the Portuguese, used it generously. I love to eat this meat dish with *chapatis* or *parathas* or *naans*. If you prefer rice, then the more moist *pullaos*, such as Mushroom *Pullao* (page 199), would be the perfect accompaniment. You could also make this dish with stewing lamb from the shoulder.

Serves 4 to 6

6 tablespoons vegetable oil

900 g (2 lb) boneless stewing beef from the neck and shoulder, cut into 4 cm (1½ inch) cubes

225 g (8 oz) onions, peeled and very finely chopped

6 cloves garlic, peeled and very finely chopped

½ teaspoon powdered ginger

⅛ –½ teaspoon cayenne pepper

1 tablespoon paprika

2 teaspoons salt

½ teaspoon very coarsely ground black pepper

300 ml (10 fl oz) natural yoghurt, beaten lightly

Pre-heat the oven to 180°C/350°F/Gas 4.

Put the oil in a wide, flameproof casserole-type pan and set over medium-high heat. When hot, put in as many meat pieces as the pan will hold easily in a single layer. Brown the meat pieces on all sides and set them aside in a deep plate. Brown all the meat this way.

Put the onions and garlic into the same pan and turn the heat down to medium. Stir and fry the onion-garlic mixture for about 10 minutes or until it has browned. Now put in the browned meat as well as any juices that might have accumulated in the plate. Also put in the ginger, cayenne, paprika, salt and black pepper. Stir for a minute. Now put in the yoghurt and bring to a simmer. Cover tightly, first with aluminium foil and then with a lid, and bake in the oven for 1½ hours. The meat should be tender by now. If it is not tender, pour in 150 ml (5 fl oz) boiling water, cover tightly, and bake another 20–30 minutes or until the meat is tender. Stir the meat gently before serving.

red lamb or beef stew

Rogan josh

Rogan josh gets its name from its rich, red appearance. The red appearance, in turn, is derived from ground red chillies, which are used quite generously in this recipe. If you want your dish to have the right colour and not be very hot, combine paprika with cayenne pepper in any proportion that you like. Just make sure that your paprika is fresh and has a good red colour. There are many recipes for *rogan josh*. This is probably the simplest of them all. It may be served with an Indian bread or rice. A green bean or aubergine dish would be a perfect accompaniment.

Serves 4 to 6

Two 2.5 cm (1 inch) cubes fresh ginger, peeled and coarsely chopped

8 cloves garlic, peeled

4 tablespoons plus 300–450 ml (10–15 fl oz) water

10 tablespoons vegetable oil

900 g (2 lb) boned lamb from the shoulder or leg, or stewing beef (chuck), cut into 2.5 cm (1 inch) cubes

10 cardamom pods

2 bay leaves

6 cloves

10 peppercorns

2.5 cm (1 inch) cinnamon stick

200 g (7 oz) onions, peeled and finely chopped

1 teaspoon ground coriander

2 teaspoons ground cumin

4 teaspoons bright red paprika mixed with $^{1}/_{4}$–1 teaspoon cayenne pepper

$1^{1}/_{4}$ teaspoons salt

6 tablespoons natural yoghurt

$^{1}/_{4}$ teaspoon *garam masala* (page 21)

Freshly ground black pepper

Put the ginger, garlic, and 4 tablespoons water into the container of an electric blender. Blend well until you have a smooth paste.

Heat the oil in a wide, heavy pan over medium-high heat. Brown the meat cubes in several batches and set to one side. Put the cardamom pods, bay leaves, cloves, peppercorns and cinnamon into the same hot oil. Stir once and wait until the cloves swell and the bay leaves begin to take on colour. This just takes a few seconds. Now put in the onions. Stir and fry for about 5 minutes or until the onions turn a medium-brown colour. Put in the ginger-garlic paste and stir for 30 seconds. Then add the coriander, cumin, paprika-cayenne and salt. Stir and fry for another 30 seconds. Add the fried meat cubes and juices. Stir for 30 seconds. Now put in 1 tablespoon of the yoghurt. Stir and fry for about 30 seconds or until the yoghurt is well blended. Add the remaining yoghurt, a tablespoon at a time as before. Stir and fry for 3–4 minutes.

Now add 300 ml (10 fl oz) water if you are cooking lamb and 450 ml (15 fl oz) water if you are cooking beef. Bring the contents of the pan to a boil, scraping in all browned spices on the sides and bottom of the pan. Cover, turn heat to low and simmer for about an hour for lamb and 2 hours for beef, or until the meat is tender. (It could be baked, covered, in a pre-heated 180°C/350°F/Gas 4 oven for the same length of time or until tender.) Every 10 minutes or so, give the meat a good stir. When the meat is tender, take off the lid, turn the heat up to medium, and boil away some of the liquid. You should end up with tender meat in a thick, reddish-brown sauce. Spoon off the fat. Sprinkle *garam masala* and black pepper over the meat before you serve and mix them in.

mughlai lamb with turnips
Shabdeg

Turnips are perhaps the most underrated vegetable in the world. This classical Mogul recipe calls for small, whole turnips. The turnips end up by absorbing all the delicious meat juices, turning buttery soft and yet retaining their own rather pretty shape. I like to serve this dish with Mushroom *Pullao* (page 199) and Spicy Green Beans (page 132). *Dal* and a yoghurt relish can also be added to the meal.

Serves 6

10 small turnips, weighing 750 g
(1½ lb) without leaves and stems
(if your turnips are larger, halve them)

2 teaspoons salt

450 g (1 lb) onions, peeled

8 tablespoons vegetable oil

1 kg (2¼ lb) stewing lamb (with bone)
from the shoulder, cut into 4 cm
(1½ inch) cubes

300 ml (10 fl oz) natural yoghurt

2.5 cm (1 inch) piece fresh ginger, peeled
and very finely chopped

½ teaspoon ground turmeric

½ teaspoon cayenne pepper

1 tablespoon ground coriander

2.25 litres (4 pints) water

½ teaspoon *garam masala* (page 21)

Peel the turnips and prick them all over with a fork. Put them in a bowl and rub them with ¾ teaspoon of the salt. Set aside for 1½–2 hours.

Cut the onions in half, lengthwise, and then crosswise into very thin slices.

Put the oil in a large, wide and preferably non-stick pan over medium-high heat. When hot, put in the onions. Stir and fry for about 12 minutes or until the onions are a reddish-brown colour. Remove the onions with a slotted spoon, squeezing out and leaving behind as much oil as you can. Spread the onions out on a plate. Put the meat into the same pan. Also put in the yoghurt, ginger and 1 teaspoon of the salt. Stir and bring to a boil. Turn the heat up high. You should, at this stage, have a fair amount of rather thin sauce. Cook on high heat, stirring every now and then, for about 10 minutes or until the sauce is fairly thick and you just begin to see the oil. Turn the heat down a bit to medium-high and continue to stir and fry for 5–7 minutes or until the meat is lightly browned and the sauce has disappeared. Turn the heat to medium-low. Put in the turmeric, cayenne and coriander. Stir for a minute.

Now put in the water and 1 teaspoon of the salt. Drain the turnips and add them as well. Bring the pan to a boil. Turn the heat to medium-high and continue to cook, uncovered, for about 45 minutes or until you have less than a third of the liquid left.

Stir the pan several times during this cooking period.

Put in the browned onions and the *garam masala*. Stir gently to mix and turn heat to low. Cook gently, uncovered, for another 10 minutes. Stir a few times during this period, taking care not to break the turnips.

Spoon off the oil that floats to the top and serve hot.

goan-style hot and sour pork

Vindaloo

The Hindus and Muslims of India do not, generally, eat pork – but Indian Christians do. This dish, with its semi-Portuguese name suggesting that the meat is cooked with wine (or vinegar) and garlic, is a contribution from the Konkani-speaking Christians of western India.

Vindaloos, which may be made out of lamb and beef as well, are usually very, very hot. You can control this heat by putting in just as many red chillies as you think you can manage. Serve mounds of fluffy rice on the side.

Serves 6

2 teaspoons cumin seeds

2–3 dried, hot red chillies

1 teaspoon black peppercorns

1 teaspoon cardamom seeds (you may take the seeds out of the pods if you cannot buy them loose)

7.5 cm (3 inch) cinnamon stick

1½ teaspoons black mustard seeds

1 teaspoon fenugreek seeds

5 tablespoons white wine vinegar

1½–2 teaspoons salt

1 teaspoon light brown sugar

10 tablespoons vegetable oil

175–200 g (6–7 oz) onions, peeled and sliced into fine half-rings

4–6 tablespoons plus 250 ml (8 fl oz) water

900 g (2 lb) boneless pork from the shoulder, cut into 2.5 cm (1 inch) cubes

2.5 cm (1 inch) cube fresh ginger, peeled and coarsely chopped

1 small, whole head of garlic, with all the cloves separated and peeled (or the equivalent, if using a large head)

1 tablespoon ground coriander

½ teaspoon ground turmeric

Grind the cumin seeds, red chillies, peppercorns, cardamom seeds, cinnamon, black mustard seeds and fenugreek seeds in a coffee-grinder or other spice-grinder. Put the ground spices in a bowl. Add the vinegar, salt and sugar. Mix and set aside.

Put the oil in a wide, heavy pan and set over medium heat. Put in the onions. Fry, stirring frequently, until the onions turn brown and crisp. Remove the onions with a slotted spoon and put them into the container of an electric blender or food processor. (Turn the heat off.) Add 2–3 tablespoons water to the blender and purée the onions. Add this purée to the ground spices in the bowl. (This is the *vindaloo* paste.) It may be made ahead of time and frozen.

Dry off the meat cubes with kitchen paper and remove large pieces of fat, if any.

Put the ginger and garlic into the container of an electric blender or food processor. Add 2–3 tablespoons water and blend until you have a smooth paste.

Heat the oil remaining in the pan once again over medium-high heat. When hot, put in the pork cubes, a few at a time, and brown them lightly on all sides. Remove each batch with a slotted spoon and keep in a bowl. Do all the pork this way. Now put the ginger-garlic paste into the same pan. Turn down the heat to medium. Stir the paste for a few seconds. Add the coriander and turmeric. Stir for another few seconds. Add the meat, any juices that may have accumulated as well as the *vindaloo* paste and 250 ml (8 fl oz) water. Bring to a boil. Cover and simmer gently for an hour or until pork is tender. Stir a few times during this cooking period.

pork chops with chick peas

Chhole wala gosht

Normally, this hearty, stew-type dish is cooked with cubes of pork cut off from the shoulder. I have substituted the more easily available thin-cut pork chops and added some mushrooms for good measure.

In India, we often ate this dish with what was pronounced as 'selice' and was, in reality, *slices* of white bread. (As a child, I had assumed that 'selice' was just another Indian word!) I now prefer slices from the crustier French loaf. Beside the bread, you need to serve nothing more than a simple vegetable, cooked in an Indian or English style. A simple salad would also do. This is a perfect dish for a winter's day and is best served in individual bowls or soup plates.

Dried chick peas can be cooked in many ways. You can soak them overnight before cooking them or you can follow the method that I have used here which allows the entire dish to be made in the course of a single day.

You may make these pork chops a day ahead of time and just reheat them.

Serves 6

225 g (8 oz) dried chick peas, picked over, rinsed and drained

1.75 litres (3 pints) plus 3 tablespoons water

4 cm (1½ inch) cube fresh ginger, peeled and coarsely chopped

5 cloves garlic, peeled

4 tablespoons vegetable oil

900 g (2 lb) thin-cut pork chops (sometimes called 'breakfast chops')

8 cardamom pods

2.5 cm (1 inch) cinnamon stick

2 bay leaves

1 teaspoon cumin seeds

175 g (6 oz) onions, peeled and coarsely chopped

1 tablespoon ground cumin

1 tablespoon ground coriander

1 teaspoon ground turmeric

300 g (11 oz) tomatoes, peeled (page 30) and chopped

350 g (12 oz) potatoes, peeled and cut into 2 cm (¾ inch) dice

1 tablespoon salt

275 g (10 oz) medium-sized mushrooms, halved

½ teaspoon cayenne pepper (use more or less as desired)

Put the chick peas in a pan. Add 1.75 litres (3 pints) water and bring to a boil. Cover, turn heat to low and simmer for 2 minutes. Turn off the heat and let the pan sit, covered, for 1 hour. Bring the chick peas to a boil again. Cover, turn heat to low and simmer for 1½ hours.

Put the ginger, garlic and 3 tablespoons water into the container of a food processor or blender. Blend until you have a paste.

Put the oil in a large, wide pan and set over medium-high heat. When hot, put in as many pork chops as the pan will hold in a single layer. Brown them on both sides without attempting to cook them through. Remove the chops and put them on a plate.

Put the cardamom pods, cinnamon, bay leaves and cumin seeds into the hot oil. Immediately, turn the heat down to medium low. Stir once and put in the onions. Stir and fry the onions for a minute, scraping the hardened pan juices as you do so. Now put in the ginger-garlic paste and stir once. Put in the ground cumin, ground coriander and turmeric. Stir for a minute. Put in the tomatoes, potatoes, pork chops and any liquid that may have accumulated in the plate, salt, and the chick peas and all their cooking liquid. Stir and bring to a boil. Cover, turn heat to low and simmer for 45 minutes. Add the mushrooms and cayenne. Cover and simmer for 15 minutes.

Note: The large whole spices in this dish should not be eaten.

Since chicken is now mass produced and fairly cheap, its status has been greatly reduced. This saddens me. I was brought up thinking of chicken as something special and have never managed to get over thinking so; besides, I like chicken. And there are such wonderful ways to cook it, from the simple Spicy Baked Chicken to the elegant *Makkhani murghi* (Chicken in a Butter Sauce) and the very impressive *Murgh musallam* (Whole Chicken Baked in Aluminium Foil). If you are on a diet, you can eat Tandoori-style Chicken which is cooked without fat and when you want to indulge yourself, you can dine on *Shahjahani murghi* (Mughlai Chicken with Almonds and Sultanas).

There are two things to remember when cooking Indian-style chicken dishes. The first is that we nearly always skin the chicken before we cook it. Skin has never been popular in India, perhaps because it gets so soft and flabby in stews. The second is that, for most of our dishes, we cut up the chicken into fairly small pieces. Legs, for example, are always separated into drumsticks and thighs. Breasts are cut into 4–6 parts. Wings and backs are similarly cut up.

When one of my recipes calls for chicken pieces, you can either buy a whole 1.5 kg (3–3½ lb) chicken and cut it up yourself using a sharp knife and a cleaver or else you can buy chicken joints – the ones you prefer – and cut them up further, if necessary. I happen to have a family in which four members like dark meat and one only likes breast meat (unless it is a roast, when we all prefer breast meat). This does not make life easy. But I do have to keep everyone happy so I frequently resort to buying joints.

poultry and eggs

bombay-style chicken with red split lentils

Murghi aur masoor dal

This dish is really like a hearty stew, just perfect for cold winter days. You could add vegetables such as shelled peas or 1 cm (½ inch) lengths of green beans. Put them in when you add the lemon juice. Traditionally, rice is served on the side but you could serve thickly cut slices of some dark, crusty bread.

Serves 6 to 7

250 g (9 oz) red split lentils (*masoor dal*), picked over, washed and drained

75 g (3 oz) onions, peeled and chopped

½ –1 fresh, hot green chilli, finely sliced

2 teaspoons ground cumin

½ teaspoon ground turmeric

1 teaspoon peeled, very finely chopped ginger

1.5 litres (2½ pints) water

About 1.5 kg (3 lb) chicken pieces, skinned

2¼ teaspoons salt

2 tablespoons vegetable oil

1 teaspoon cumin seeds

2–4 cloves garlic, peeled and finely chopped

¼ –¾ teaspoon cayenne pepper

2 tablespoons lemon juice

½ teaspoon sugar

¼ teaspoon *garam masala* (page 21)

Optional garnish: 3 tablespoons chopped, fresh green coriander

Combine the lentils, onions, green chilli, ground cumin, turmeric, half of the chopped ginger and the water in a big, heavy pan. Bring to a simmer, cover, leaving the lid very slightly ajar, and cook on low heat for 45 minutes. Add the chicken pieces and the salt. Mix and bring to a boil. Cover, turn heat to low and simmer gently for 25–30 minutes or until the chicken is tender.

Put the oil in a small frying-pan and set over medium heat. When hot, put in the cumin seeds. As soon as the seeds begin to sizzle – this just takes a few seconds – put in the remaining ½ teaspoon chopped ginger and the garlic. Fry until the garlic turns slightly brown. Now put in the cayenne. Lift up the frying-pan immediately and pour its entire contents – oil and spices – into the pan with the chicken and lentils. Also add the lemon juice, sugar and *garam masala*. Stir to mix and cook on medium-low heat for 5 minutes.

Sprinkle the fresh coriander over the top, if you wish, just before you serve.

tandoori-style chicken

Tandoori murghi

I have, I think, found a way to make tandoori-style chicken without a *tandoor*! The *tandoor*, as I am sure you all know by now, is a vat-shaped clay oven, heated with charcoal or wood. The heat inside builds up to such an extent that small whole chickens, skewered and thrust into it, cook in about 10 minutes. This fierce heat seals the juices of the bird and keeps it moist while an earlier marinating process ensures that the chicken is tender and well flavoured. The result is quite spectacular.

To approximate a *tandoor*, I use an ordinary oven, pre-heated to its maximum temperature. Then, instead of cooking a whole bird, I use serving-sized pieces – legs that are cut into two and breasts that are quartered. The cooking time is not 10 minutes because home ovens do not get as hot as *tandoors*. Still, breasts cook in about 15–20 minutes and legs in 20–25 minutes.

Tandoori chicken may, of course, be served just the way it comes out of the oven with a few wedges of lemon, or it can, without much effort, be transformed into *Makkhani murghi* (see next recipe) by smothering it with a rich butter-cream-tomato sauce. Both dishes are excellent for dinner parties as most of the work can be done a day ahead of time. The chicken is marinated the night before so all you have to do on the day of the party is to cook it in the oven for a brief 20–25 minutes just before you sit down to eat. If you wish to make the sauce, all the ingredients for it except the butter may be combined in a bowl the day before and refrigerated. After that, the sauce cooks in less than 5 minutes and involves only one step – heating it.

Both these chicken dishes may be served with rice or *naan* and a green bean or cauliflower dish.

Note: The traditional orange colour of cooked tandoori chicken comes from food colouring. You may or may not want to use it. If you do, mix yellow and red liquid food colours to get a bright orange shade. If your red is very dark, use only ½ tablespoon of it.

Serves 4 to 6

1.25 kg (2½ lb) chicken pieces, skinned (you may use legs, breasts or a combination of the two)

1 teaspoon salt

1 juicy lemon

450 ml (15 fl oz) natural yoghurt

½ medium-sized onion, peeled and quartered

1 clove garlic, peeled

2 cm (¾ inch) cube fresh ginger, peeled and quartered

½ fresh, hot green chilli, roughly sliced

2 teaspoons *garam masala* (page 21)

3 tablespoons yellow liquid food colouring mixed with ½–1½ tablespoons red liquid food colouring (optional, see opposite)

Lime wedges (optional)

Cut each leg into 2 pieces and each breast into 4 pieces. Cut 2 long slits on each side of each part of the legs. The slits should never start at an edge and they should be deep enough to reach the bone. Cut similar slits on the meaty side of each breast piece.

Spread the chicken pieces out on one or two large platters. Sprinkle half the salt and squeeze the juice from three-quarters of the lemon over them. Lightly rub the salt and lemon juice into the slits. Turn the chicken pieces over and do the same on the other side with the remaining salt and lemon juice. Set aside for 20 minutes.

Combine the yoghurt, onion, garlic, ginger, green chilli and *garam masala* in the container of an electric blender or food processor. Blend until you have a smooth paste. Empty the paste into a sieve set over a large ceramic or stainless-steel bowl. Push the paste through.

Brush the chicken pieces on both sides with the food colouring and then put them with any accumulated juices and any remaining food colouring into the bowl with the marinade. Mix well, making sure that the marinade goes into the slits in the chicken. Cover and refrigerate for 6–24 hours (the longer the better). Pre-heat the oven to its maximum temperature.

Take the chicken pieces out of the bowl, shaking off as much of the marinade as possible. Arrange them in a large shallow baking tray in a single layer. Bake for 20–25 minutes or until just done. You might test the chicken with a fork just to be sure. Serve hot, with lime wedges if you wish.

Note: The left-over marinade may be frozen and re-used *once*.

mughlai chicken with almonds and sultanas

Shahjahani murghi

This elegant, mild dish is very suitable for dinner parties. It could be accompanied by Spiced Basmati Rice (page 194), Cauliflower with Potatoes (page 144), and Yoghurt with Walnuts and Fresh Coriander (page 211).

Serves 6

2.5 cm (1 inch) cube fresh ginger, peeled and coarsely chopped

8–9 cloves garlic, peeled

6 tablespoons blanched, slivered almonds

4 tablespoons water

7 tablespoons vegetable oil

1.5 kg (3 lb) chicken pieces, skinned

10 cardamom pods

2.5 cm (1 inch) cinnamon stick

2 bay leaves

5 cloves

200 g (7 oz) onions, peeled and finely chopped

2 teaspoons ground cumin

$1/8$–$1/2$ teaspoon cayenne pepper

7 tablespoons natural yoghurt

300 ml (10 fl oz) single cream

$1^{1}/_{2}$ teaspoons salt

1–2 tablespoons sultanas

$1/4$ teaspoon *garam masala* (page 21)

Put the ginger, garlic, 4 tablespoons of the almonds and the water into the container of an electric blender and blend until you have a paste.

Put the oil in a wide, preferably non-stick, pan or deep frying-pan and set over medium-high heat. When hot, put in as many chicken pieces as the pan will hold in a single layer. Let the chicken pieces turn golden-brown on the bottom. Now turn all the pieces over and brown the second side. Remove the chicken pieces with a slotted spoon and put them in a bowl. Brown all the chicken pieces this way.

Put the cardamom pods, cinnamon, bay leaves and cloves into the same hot oil. Stir and fry them for a few seconds. Now put in the onions. Stir and fry the onions for 3–4 minutes or until they are lightly browned. Put in the paste from the blender and the cumin and cayenne. Stir and fry for 2–3 minutes or until the oil seems to separate from the spice mixture and the spices are lightly browned. Add 1 tablespoon of the yoghurt. Stir and fry it for about 30 seconds. Now add another tablespoon of yoghurt. Keep doing this until all the yoghurt has been incorporated.

Put in the chicken pieces, any liquid that might have accumulated in the chicken bowl, the cream and salt. Bring to a simmer. Cover, turn heat to low and cook gently for 20 minutes. Add the sultanas and turn over the chicken pieces. Cover and cook another 10 minutes or until the chicken is tender. Add the *garam masala*. Stir to mix.

Put the remaining almonds on a baking tray and put them under the grill until they brown lightly. You have to toss them frequently. Sprinkle these almonds over the chicken when you serve. Extra fat may be spooned off the top just before serving.

Note: The whole spices in this dish should not be eaten.

chicken with cream

Malai wali murghi

This rich, creamy dish may be served with Aubergine Cooked in the Pickling Style
(page 136) and rice.

Serves 6

1½ teaspoons salt

2 teaspoons ground cumin

1½ teaspoons ground coriander

½ teaspoon ground turmeric

½ teaspoon cayenne pepper

Freshly ground black pepper

1.5 kg (3 lb) chicken pieces, skinned

6–7 cloves garlic, peeled

2.5 cm (1 inch) cube fresh ginger,
peeled and coarsely chopped

320 ml (11 fl oz) water

6 tablespoons vegetable oil

100 g (4 oz) onions, peeled and
finely chopped

175 g (6 oz) tomatoes, peeled (page 30)
and finely chopped

4 tablespoons natural yoghurt

1 teaspoon *garam masala* (page 21)

6 tablespoons double cream

Sprinkle ½ teaspoon of the salt, 1 teaspoon of the cumin, ½ teaspoon of the
coriander, ¼ teaspoon of the turmeric, ¼ teaspoon of the cayenne and some
black pepper on the chicken pieces. Mix well and set aside for at least 1 hour.

Put the garlic and ginger into the container of an electric blender or food
processor. Add 120 ml (4 fl oz) of the water and blend until fairly smooth.

Put the oil in a wide, preferably non-stick, pan and set over medium-high heat.
When hot, put in as many chicken pieces as the pan will hold easily in a single
layer and brown lightly on both sides. Remove with a slotted spoon and set
aside in a bowl. Brown all the chicken pieces the same way.

Put the chopped onions into the remaining oil. Stir and fry until the pieces turn
a medium-brown colour. Add the garlic-ginger paste. Stir and fry until all the
water from the paste evaporates and you see the oil again. Put in the remaining
1 teaspoon cumin, 1 teaspoon coriander, ¼ teaspoon turmeric, and ¼ teaspoon
cayenne. Stir and fry for about 20 seconds. Now put in the chopped tomatoes.
Turn the heat down to medium-low. Stir and cook the spice paste for
3–4 minutes, mashing the tomato pieces with the back of a slotted spoon as you
do so. Add the yoghurt, a tablespoon at a time, incorporating it into the sauce
each time before you add any more. Put in the chicken pieces and any
accumulated juices, the remaining 200 ml (7 fl oz) water and 1 teaspoon salt.
Bring to a boil. Cover, turn heat to low and simmer for 20 minutes. Take off the
cover. Add the *garam masala* and cream. Mix gently.

Turn the heat up to medium-high and cook, stirring gently every now and then,
until the sauce has reduced somewhat and has turned fairly thick.

chicken with tomatoes and garam masala

Timatar murghi

This simple chicken dish used to be a great favourite with our children. I generally serve it with Plain Long-grain Rice (page 192) and Whole Green Lentils with Garlic and Onion (page 167).

Serves 6

5 tablespoons vegetable oil

¾ teaspoon cumin seeds

2.5 cm (1 inch) cinnamon stick

6 cardamom pods

2 bay leaves

¼ teaspoon peppercorns

175 g (6 oz) onions, peeled and finely chopped

6–7 cloves garlic, peeled and finely chopped

2.5 cm (1 inch) cube fresh ginger, peeled and finely chopped

450 g (1 lb) fresh tomatoes, peeled (page 30) and finely chopped (canned tomatoes may be substituted)

1.5 kg (3 lb) chicken pieces, skinned

1½ teaspoons salt

⅛–½ teaspoon cayenne pepper

½ teaspoon *garam masala* (page 21)

Put the oil in a large, wide pan and set over medium-high heat. When hot, put in the cumin seeds, cinnamon, cardamom pods, bay leaves and peppercorns. Stir once and then put in the onions, garlic and ginger. Stir this mixture around until the onions pick up brown specks. Now put in the tomatoes, chicken pieces, salt and cayenne pepper. Stir to mix and bring to a boil. Cover tightly, turn heat to low and simmer for 25 minutes or until the chicken is tender. Stir a few times during this cooking period. Remove cover and turn up heat to medium.

Sprinkle in the *garam masala* and cook, stirring gently, for about 5 minutes in order to reduce the liquid in the pan somewhat.

Note: The whole spices in this dish should not be eaten.

goan-style chicken with roasted coconut

Shakoothi

I just love this dish. I ate it for the first time in balmy, palm-fringed, coastal Goa, and have been hoarding the recipe ever since. Even though there are several steps to the recipe, it is not at all hard to put together, especially if you have grated coconut sitting around in the freezer, as I always have. I am now in the habit of buying two or three coconuts whenever I see any good ones. I grate them as soon as I get home (for instructions, see page 18) and then store the grated flesh in flattened plastic packets. Defrosting takes no time at all. This way, I am always ready, not only to make *shakoothi*, but to sprinkle fresh coconut over meats and vegetables whenever I want to.

You could serve this dish with Plain Long-grain Rice (page 192), Spicy Green Beans (page 132) and Onion Relish (page 221).

Serves 4 to 5

1½ tablespoons coriander seeds

1½ teaspoons cumin seeds

1 teaspoon black mustard seeds

2.5 cm (1 inch) cinnamon stick, broken into 3–4 pieces

4 cloves

¼ teaspoon black peppercorns

About ⅙ nutmeg

1 dried, hot red chilli (remove seeds if you want it mild)

Enough grated fresh coconut (see page 18) to fill a measuring jug to the 450 ml (15 fl oz) level

6–8 cloves garlic, peeled

2.5 cm (1 inch) cube fresh ginger, peeled and coarsely chopped

½–1 fresh, hot green chilli

4 tablespoons plus 300 ml (10 fl oz) water

4 tablespoons vegetable oil

175 g (6 oz) onions, peeled and minced

1 kg (2¼ lb) chicken pieces, skinned

1½ teaspoons salt

Put the coriander seeds, cumin seeds, mustard seeds, cinnamon, cloves, peppercorns, nutmeg and red chilli in a small, preferably cast-iron frying-pan. Place the pan over medium heat. Now quickly 'dry-roast' the spices, stirring them frequently until they emit a very pleasant 'roasted' aroma. Empty the spices into a clean coffee-grinder or spice-grinder and grind until fine. Take the spices out and put them in a bowl.

Put the coconut into the same frying-pan and dry-roast it over medium heat, stirring it all the time. The coconut should pick up lots of brown flecks and also smell 'roasted'. Put the coconut in the bowl with the other dry-roasted spices.

Put the garlic, ginger and green chilli into the container of an electric blender, along with 4 tablespoons water. Blend until you have a paste.

Put the oil in a 25–30 cm (10–12 inch) frying-pan or sauté pan and set over medium-high heat. When hot, put in the onions. Stir and fry them until they pick up brown spots. Now pour in the garlic-ginger mixture from the blender and stir once. Turn heat to medium. Put in the chicken pieces and salt, as well as the spice-coconut mixture in the bowl. Stir and fry the chicken for 3–4 minutes or until it loses its pinkness and turns slightly brown. Add 300 ml (10 fl oz) water and bring to a simmer. Cover tightly, turn heat to low, and cook for 25–30 minutes or until the chicken is tender. Stir a few times during this cooking period, making sure that you turn over each piece of chicken so that it gets evenly coloured.

chicken in a red sweet pepper sauce

Lal masale wali murghi

Many of the meat, poultry and fish dishes which are traditional along India's west coast have thick and stunningly red-looking sauces. The main ingredient, which provides both the texture and the colour, is red chillies – fresh or dried. It is almost impossible to find the correct variety of red chilli in the West – one that is bright red and just mildly hot. What I have discovered, is that a combination of red peppers and cayenne pepper works exceedingly well!

I like to serve this dish with Aromatic Yellow Rice (page 200) and Yoghurt with Aubergines (page 212).

Serves 4

1 kg (2¼ lb) chicken pieces

100 g (4 oz) onions, peeled and coarsely chopped

2.5 cm (1 inch) cube fresh ginger, peeled and coarsely chopped

3 cloves garlic, peeled

25 g (1 oz) blanched, slivered almonds

350 g (12 oz) red sweet peppers, trimmed, seeded and coarsely chopped

1 tablespoon ground cumin

2 teaspoons ground coriander

½ teaspoon ground turmeric

⅛ – ½ teaspoon cayenne pepper

2 teaspoons salt

7 tablespoons vegetable oil

250 ml (8 fl oz) water

2 tablespoons lemon juice

½ teaspoon coarsely ground black pepper

If chicken legs are whole, divide drumsticks from thighs with a sharp knife. Breasts should be cut into 4 parts. Skin all chicken pieces.

Combine the onions, ginger, garlic, almonds, peppers, cumin, coriander, turmeric, cayenne and salt in the container of a food processor or blender. Blend, pushing down with a rubber spatula whenever you need to, until you have a paste.

Put the oil in a large, wide, preferably non-stick, pan and set over medium-high heat. When hot, pour in all the paste. Stir and fry it for 10–12 minutes or until you see the oil forming tiny bubbles around it.

Put in the chicken, with the water, lemon juice and black pepper. Stir to mix and bring to a boil. Cover, turn heat to low and simmer gently for 25 minutes or until the chicken is tender. Stir a few times.

chicken with roasted coriander in a coconut curry sauce

Dakshini murgh

Here I have combined roasted seeds – coriander, fenugreek and black pepper –
with coconut milk to make a Southern-style chicken. It has a goodly amount of delicious
sauce, so eat it with rice and a vegetable of your choice. This is an ideal dish for
entertaining. You could easily make it part of a more elaborate menu.

Serves 4

3 tablespoons coriander seeds

¼ teaspoon fenugreek seeds

2 teaspoons black peppercorns

6 tablespoons vegetable oil

1 teaspoon black mustard seeds

5 cm (2 inch) cinnamon stick

1.5 kg (3½ lb) chicken pieces, skinned
and cut into small serving portions

2 medium-sized onions, peeled
and cut into fine half-rings

4–5 cloves garlic, peeled and
cut into fine slivers

1 teaspoon peeled, very finely grated
fresh ginger

100–150 g (4–5 oz) tomatoes,
finely chopped

½ teaspoon ground turmeric

1 teaspoon cayenne pepper

1½ teaspoons salt

1 tablespoon lemon juice

One 400 g (14 oz) can of coconut milk

2 fresh, hot green chillies,
split in half, lengthwise

Set a small, cast-iron frying-pan over medium-high heat for 2–3 minutes.
Now put the coriander seeds, fenugreek seeds and peppercorns into it. Stir and
roast them for about 1½ minutes or until they are lightly browned and emit a
roasted aroma. Remove the spices, leave them to cool slightly then grind them
finely in a clean coffee-grinder or other spice-grinder.

Put the oil in a wide, preferably non-stick, pan and set over medium-high heat.
When hot, put in the black mustard seeds and cinnamon. As soon as the
mustard seeds begin to pop – this takes just a few seconds – put in the chicken
pieces, only as many as the pan can hold easily in a single layer. Brown the
chicken pieces in as many batches as necessary and remove to a bowl.

Once all the chicken is browned, put the onions and garlic into the same pan
and turn heat to medium. Stir and fry until the onions are light brown. Now put
in the ginger and tomatoes. Stir and cook until the tomatoes are soft. Turn heat
down. Add the roasted spice mixture, turmeric, cayenne, salt and lemon juice.
Remove the very thick coconut cream that will have congealed at the top of
the coconut milk can and set aside. Stir the remaining contents of the can.
Add enough water to fill the can again and pour this mixture over the chicken.
Bring to a boil. Cover, turn heat to low and simmer for 25 minutes, stirring
now and then.

Stir the thick coconut cream that you removed and add that and the green
chillies to the chicken. Stir once or twice as the cream warms through. Turn off
the heat.

Note: The green chillies may be left as a garnish or eaten by those who are
up to it.

whole chicken baked in aluminium foil

Murgh musallam

Over the years, as I am more and more rushed for time, I find myself simplifying some of my own recipes. The traditional *murgh musallam* recipe, for example, is quite a complicated one. I now cook it relatively simply, by smothering a marinated bird with a spice paste, wrapping it in foil and popping it into the oven. It works beautifully.

I like to serve this dish with Mushroom *Pullao* (page 199), Spinach Cooked with Onions (page 156) and Yoghurt with Cucumber and Mint (page 210).

Serves 4 to 6

FOR THE MARINADE

2.5 cm (1 inch) cube fresh ginger, peeled and coarsely chopped

2 large cloves garlic, peeled

6 tablespoons natural yoghurt

$\frac{1}{2}$ teaspoon ground turmeric

$1\frac{1}{4}$ teaspoons salt

$\frac{1}{4}$–$\frac{1}{2}$ teaspoon cayenne pepper

Freshly ground black pepper

YOU ALSO NEED

One 1.5 kg ($3\frac{1}{2}$ lb) chicken

225 g (8 oz) onions

4 cloves garlic, peeled

4 cm ($1\frac{1}{2}$ inch) cube fresh ginger, peeled and coarsely chopped

25 g (1 oz) blanched, slivered almonds

2 teaspoons ground cumin

2 teaspoons ground coriander

$\frac{1}{2}$ teaspoon ground turmeric

1 tablespoon paprika

$\frac{1}{4}$ teaspoon cayenne pepper

$1\frac{1}{2}$ teaspoons salt

8 tablespoons vegetable oil

2 tablespoons lemon juice

$\frac{1}{2}$ teaspoon coarsely ground black pepper

$\frac{1}{2}$ teaspoon *garam masala* (page 21)

Make the marinade: Put the ginger, garlic and 3 tablespoons of the yoghurt into the container of a food processor or electric blender. Blend, pushing down with a rubber spatula whenever you need to, until you have a paste. Add the turmeric, salt, cayenne and black pepper. Blend for a second to mix. Empty the marinade into a bowl. (Do not wash out the food processor or blender yet.) Add the remaining 3 tablespoons of the yoghurt to the marinade and beat it in with a fork.

Skin the entire chicken with the exception of the wing tips. Skin the neck. Put the chicken, breast up, on a platter and put the giblets somewhere near it. Rub the chicken, inside and out, as well as the giblets, with the marinade. Set aside, unrefrigerated, for 2 hours.

Meanwhile, put the onions, garlic, ginger and almonds into the food processor or blender. Blend, pushing down with a rubber spatula whenever you need to, until you have a paste. Add the cumin, coriander, turmeric, paprika, cayenne and salt. Blend again to mix.

Put the oil in a large, non-stick pan and set over medium-high heat. When hot, put in the paste from the food processor or blender. Fry, stirring, for 8–9 minutes. Add the lemon juice, black pepper and *garam masala*. Mix. Turn off the heat and let the paste cool.

Pre-heat the oven to 180°C/350°F/Gas 4.

When the chicken has finished sitting in its marinade for 2 hours, spread out a piece of aluminium foil, large enough to enclose the chicken. Put the chicken, breast up, in the centre of the foil and put the giblets somewhere near it. Rub the chicken, inside and out, as well as the giblets, with the fried spice paste. Bring the ends of the foil towards the centre to form a tight packet. All 'seams' should be 5 cm (2 inches) above the 'floor' of the packet.

Put the wrapped chicken, breast up, on a baking tray and bake in the oven for $1\frac{1}{2}$ hours or until the chicken is tender.

turkey kebabs

Turkey ke kabab

Kebabs can be made out of almost any meat. As turkey is so easily available and is lower in saturated fat than many red meats, I have taken to using it at least once or twice a month.

These kebabs are best put into pockets of pitta bread along with Fresh Coriander Chutney (page 218), some sliced onions and tomatoes and a squeeze of lemon juice, or wrapped in *parathas*. They are an ideal food to take on picnics. If you wish to serve them with drinks make the patties much smaller.

Makes 6 kebabs

450 g (1 lb) finely minced turkey (put twice through the mincer)

12 tablespoons fine, dry breadcrumbs

3/4 teaspoon salt

3/4 teaspoon *garam masala* (page 21)

1/2 teaspoon cumin seeds

1/2 teaspoon coriander seeds

8 tablespoons finely chopped, fresh green coriander

2–3 fresh, hot green chillies, finely chopped

50 g (2 oz) onion, peeled and finely chopped

2 teaspoons peeled, finely grated fresh ginger

50 g (2 oz) finely chopped fresh tomato

1/4 –1/2 teaspoon cayenne pepper

Vegetable oil to line the bottom of a frying-pan

Lemon wedges

Combine the turkey, 4 tablespoons of the breadcrumbs, salt, *garam masala*, cumin seeds, coriander seeds, fresh coriander, green chillies, onion, ginger, tomato and cayenne in a bowl. Mix well and form six 7.5 cm (3 inch) patties. Put the remaining 8 tablespoons breadcrumbs on a plate and dip each patty in them. There should be a thin layer of crumbs on all sides. Cover and refrigerate the patties in a single layer until needed.

Put enough oil in a large frying-pan to cover the bottom lightly and set over medium-high heat. When hot, put in the patties – only as many as the pan will hold easily in a single layer. Cook for 3 minutes on each side. Turn heat to medium and cook for another 2–3 minutes on each side.

Eat the patties with generous squeezes of lemon juice.

eggs

The egg recipes in this chapter are simple and tasty, perfect for everyday cooking. If you are looking for a new, spicier approach to eggs, you could try *Ekoori*, scrambled eggs cooked with fresh green coriander and tomato, or the pie-like Parsi omelette seasoned with cumin and green chillies. Indians also know how to convert plain, hard-boiled eggs into the most delicious main courses by putting them into thick, creamy sauces or tart, vinegary ones.

spicy scrambled eggs

Ekoori

Ekoori is the Parsi name for them but scrambled eggs, cooked in a similar style, are
eaten all over India. Eat them with toast or any Indian bread.

Serves 4

3 tablespoons unsalted butter or
vegetable oil

1 small onion, peeled and finely chopped

½ teaspoon peeled, very finely
grated fresh ginger

½ –1 fresh, hot green chilli,
finely chopped

1 tablespoon very finely chopped, fresh
green coriander

⅛ teaspoon ground turmeric

½ teaspoon ground cumin

1 small tomato, peeled (page 30)
and chopped

6 large eggs, lightly beaten

Salt and freshly ground black pepper
to taste

Melt the butter in a medium-sized, preferably non-stick, frying-pan over
medium heat. Put in the onion and sauté until soft. Add the ginger, chilli, fresh
coriander, turmeric, cumin and tomato.

Stir and cook for 3–4 minutes or until the tomatoes are soft.

Put in the beaten eggs. Salt and pepper them lightly. Stir the eggs very gently
until they form soft, thick curds.

Cook the scrambled eggs to any consistency you like.

vegetable omelette
Parsi omlate

The Parsis who settled on India's west coast around the Bombay area came originally from Persia over a thousand years ago. Even though they have proudly retained their religion, Zoroastrianism, they have been unafraid to let their adopted country or, for that matter, British colonialists, influence them in their choice of dress, language, and food. The Parsi culinary tradition is unique, borrowing freely as it does from Gujeratis, Maharashtrians and the English. But there is a Persian streak in there as well. This can best be seen in the fondness for eggs and the abundance of egg dishes – eggs over fried okra, eggs over matchstick potatoes, eggs over tomato chutney – the list is long. Parsis also make all kinds of omelettes. Some are folded in the traditional way but many others are round and pie-like. The recipe here is for a pie-like omelette, filled with vegetables.

This omelette has become one of my favourite brunch dishes now. It may be served, Western-style, with a salad, French bread and white wine, or it may be served Indian-style, with a stack of *parathas* or toast, Tomato, Onion and Green Coriander Relish (page 215), and steaming hot tea.

To make this omelette properly, it really helps to have a non-stick frying-pan. The one I use measures 19 cm (7½ inches) across at the bottom, curving up to 25 cm (10 inches) across at the top. It is 5 cm (2 inches) in height. Your pan may have a somewhat different shape. It does not really matter. Just remember that the pie-shaped omelette rises slightly as it is cooking so a little space has to be left at the top. You also need a lid. If your frying-pan does not have one, use aluminium foil.

Serves 4 to 6

450 g (1 lb) courgettes

1¾ teaspoons salt, or to taste

5 tablespoons vegetable oil

100 g (4 oz) onions, peeled and
finely chopped

150 g (5 oz) potatoes, peeled and cut into
5 mm (¼ inch) dice

1–3 fresh, hot green chillies,
finely chopped

200 g (7 oz) tomatoes, chopped

1½ teaspoons ground cumin

⅛–¼ teaspoon cayenne pepper (optional)

Freshly ground black pepper

9 large eggs

3 tablespoons finely chopped, fresh green
coriander (parsley may be substituted)

¼ teaspoon baking powder

Trim and discard the ends of the courgettes and then grate them coarsely. Put the grated courgettes in a bowl. Sprinkle ¾ teaspoon of the salt over them and mix thoroughly. Set aside for 30 minutes. Squeeze all the liquid out of the grated courgettes and then separate the strands so they are no longer bunched up.

Put 3 tablespoons of the oil in a non-stick frying-pan (see opposite) over medium heat. When hot, put in the onions. Stir and fry for a minute. Now put in the potatoes and the green chillies. Stir and fry for about 5 minutes or until the potato pieces are just about tender. Add the courgettes, tomatoes, cumin, the remaining 1 teaspoon salt, cayenne, if using, and a generous amount of black pepper. Stir and cook for 2–3 minutes or until the tomato pieces are soft. **Set aside to** cool.

Break the eggs into a bowl and beat well. Empty the cooled vegetable mixture into the beaten eggs and add the fresh coriander or parsley. Stir to mix. Sprinkle in the baking powder, making sure that it is lump-free. Mix again.

Wipe out the frying-pan with a piece of kitchen paper. Pour in the remaining 2 tablespoons oil and set over low heat. When hot, pour in the egg mixture. Cover and cook on low heat for 15 minutes. Remove the cover. Now you have to turn the omelette over. Do it this way: Place a large plate over the frying-pan. Put one hand on the plate. Quickly and deftly, lift the frying-pan up with the other hand and turn it upside down over the plate. Your omelette will now be in the plate with its browned side on top. Slip it back into the frying-pan and cook it, uncovered, for 5 minutes. Invert the omelette once again on to a serving platter. The lighter side should now be on the top.

Serve hot, warm or at room temperature.

hard-boiled eggs in a spicy cream sauce

Malaidar unday

This delicious egg dish can be put together rather quickly and is just perfect for brunches, light lunches and suppers. You could serve toast on the side or, if you like, rice and a crisp salad. If you prefer to serve a more traditional Indian meal, then *parathas* or Spiced Basmati Rice (page 194) and Gujerati-style Green Beans (page 131) would be suitable accompaniments.

This recipe calls for a small amount of chicken stock. If you have some home-made stock handy, well and good. Otherwise, use stock made with a cube, but adjust your salt as cube stock can be salty.

Serves 3 to 4

3 tablespoons vegetable oil

50 g (2 oz) onion, peeled and finely chopped

2.5 cm (1 inch) cube fresh ginger, peeled and finely grated

$\frac{1}{2}$ –1 fresh, hot green chilli, finely chopped

300 ml (10 fl oz) single cream

1 tablespoon lemon juice

1 teaspoon ground, roasted cumin seeds (page 20)

$\frac{1}{8}$ teaspoon cayenne pepper

$\frac{1}{2}$ teaspoon salt

$\frac{1}{4}$ teaspoon *garam masala* (page 21)

2 teaspoons tomato purée

150 ml (5 fl oz) chicken stock

6–8 hard-boiled eggs, peeled and cut crosswise into halves

1 tablespoon finely chopped, fresh green coriander or parsley (optional)

Put the oil in a large, preferably non-stick, frying-pan and set over medium heat. When hot, put in the onion. Stir and fry the onion for about 3 minutes or until the pieces are browned at the edges. Put in the ginger and chilli. Stir and fry for a minute. Now put in the cream, lemon juice, ground, roasted cumin seeds, cayenne, salt, *garam masala,* tomato purée and chicken stock. Stir to mix thoroughly and bring to a simmer.

Put all the egg halves into the sauce in a single layer, cut side up. Spoon the sauce over them. Cook over medium heat for about 5 minutes, spooning the sauce frequently over the eggs as you do so. By this time the sauce will have become fairly thick. Put the egg halves carefully in a serving dish, cut side up, and pour the sauce over them. Garnish with fresh coriander or parsley, if you wish, sprinkling it lightly over the top.

vinegared eggs

Baida vindaloo

This vinegary, hard-boiled egg dish is almost like a pickle and perfect for taking out on picnics. It is, like all Goan-style *vindaloo* dishes, tart, hot, garlicky and just very slightly sweet. I have lessened the tartness somewhat by cooking the eggs in a mixture of vinegar and water instead of just vinegar. Use the mildest vinegar that you can find. In this recipe, you may use anywhere from six to eight eggs without having to alter any of the other ingredients.

You could serve this dish with rice or an Indian bread. Cauliflower with Potatoes (page 144) would make a nice accompaniment.

Serves 3 to 4

4 cloves garlic, peeled

2.5 cm (1 inch) cube fresh ginger,
peeled and very finely grated

1/8 – 1/2 teaspoon cayenne pepper

2 teaspoons paprika

1 1/2 teaspoons ground cumin

1 1/4 teaspoons salt

1 1/2 tablespoons brown sugar

2 tablespoons plus 150 ml (4 fl oz)
mild white vinegar

3 tablespoons vegetable oil

2.5 cm (1 inch) cinnamon stick

225 g (8 oz) onions, peeled and
finely chopped

1/2 teaspoon *garam masala* (page 21)

175 ml (6 fl oz) water

6–8 hard-boiled eggs, peeled and
cut crosswise into halves

Mash the garlic cloves to a pulp or put them through a garlic press.

Combine the garlic, ginger, cayenne, paprika, cumin, salt, brown sugar and 2 tablespoons vinegar in a cup or small bowl. Mix well.

Put the oil in a medium-sized frying-pan and set over medium heat. When hot, put in the cinnamon stick. Let it sizzle for a few seconds. Now put in all the onions. Stir and fry for about 5 minutes or until the onions have softened. Put in the paste from the cup as well as the *garam masala*. Stir and fry for 2 minutes. Add 150 ml (4 fl oz) vinegar and 175 ml (6 fl oz) water. Stir to mix and bring to a simmer. Put all the egg halves into the frying-pan in a single layer, cut side up, and spoon the sauce over them. Cook on medium heat for about 5 minutes or until the sauce has thickened. Spoon the sauce frequently over the eggs as you do so.

hard-boiled eggs cooked with potatoes

Unday aur aloo

This simple dish is quite a family favourite. We eat it with an Indian bread or plain rice. It makes a pleasant change from meat, and is economical too.

Serves 2 to 4

2 cloves garlic, peeled

2.5 cm (1 inch) cube fresh ginger, peeled and coarsely chopped

2 tablespoons plus 300 ml (10 fl oz) water

450 g (1 lb) potatoes, peeled

6 tablespoons vegetable oil

150 g (5 oz) onions, peeled and finely chopped

1/8 teaspoon cayenne pepper

1 tablespoon ground coriander

1 teaspoon plain flour

4 tablespoons natural yoghurt

300 g (11 oz) tomatoes, peeled (page 30) and finely chopped

1 1/2 teaspoons salt

1/2 teaspoon *garam masala* (page 21)

1 tablespoon very finely chopped, fresh green coriander (parsley may be substituted)

4 hard-boiled eggs, peeled

Put the garlic, ginger and 2 tablespoons water into the container of a food processor or blender and blend until you have a paste.

Cut the potatoes into 1 cm (1/2 inch) thick slices. Now cut the slices lengthwise into 1 cm (1/2 inch) wide chips.

Put the oil in a large, preferably non-stick, frying-pan and set over medium-high heat. When hot, put in the potatoes. Turn and fry them until all sides turn golden-brown. The potatoes should not cook through. Remove them with a slotted spoon and put aside on a plate.

Put the onions into the same oil. Stir and fry until they turn medium brown. Now put in the garlic-ginger paste. Stir and fry for a minute. Put in the cayenne, ground coriander and flour. Stir for a minute. Put in 1 tablespoon of the yoghurt. Stir for about 30 seconds or until it has been incorporated into the sauce. Add all the yoghurt this way, 1 tablespoon at a time. Now put in the tomatoes. Stir and fry for 2 minutes. Add 300 ml (10 fl oz) water and the salt. Bring to a boil. Cover the frying-pan, turn the heat to low and simmer for 10 minutes.

Put the potatoes into the sauce and bring to a simmer. Cover, turn heat to low and simmer for 10 minutes or until the potatoes are just tender. Add the *garam masala* and fresh coriander or parsley. Stir gently to mix.

Halve the eggs, crosswise, and carefully put them into the frying-pan with the cut sides up. Try not to let the yolks fall out. Spoon some sauce over the eggs. Bring to a simmer. Cover and simmer on low heat for 5 minutes.

There is nothing quite like good fresh fish. It is light, cooks fast and may be prepared simply and elegantly at the same time. Needless to say, the types of fish available in Indian rivers, lakes and seas are different from the ones found in the colder northern waters.

What I have done for this chapter is to work out Indian-style recipes for the fish that are commonly available in the West. The prawns I have used are the cooked, packed frozen ones that are found in supermarkets or freezer centres and fishmongers. Just look for the largest and best varieties that you can find.

Indians eat a fair amount of breaded, fried fish. I have used plaice for this as it is similar to our pomfret, at least in general shape. Our mackerel has a plumper form but is very similar in taste. So I have used it for a west coast recipe that calls for a fresh coriander and lemon marinade. We have no cod, halibut or haddock in India but they are similar in texture to some of our river fish. I have used them in Indian-style recipes in which they are cooked with tomatoes or yoghurt or cauliflower.

I have even included a recipe for mussels. This is a Goan recipe, one of the few in this book that uses fresh coconut. It is an exquisite dish that can be made either with cockles or mussels.

I need hardly repeat that if you are buying fresh fish, make sure that it is fresh. The gills should be bright red, the eyes clear, the skin shiny and the body firm and taut. The fish should not have a pronounced fishy odour.

fish

goan-style mussels

Thisra

Although they are eaten with rice in Goa, I love to serve these mussels all by
themselves as a first course.

Serves 6

30–36 small to medium-sized mussels

2.5 cm (1 inch) cube fresh ginger, peeled
and coarsely chopped

8 cloves garlic, peeled

370 ml (12 fl oz) water

4 tablespoons vegetable oil

175–200g (6–7 oz) onions, peeled
and chopped

1½–2 fresh, hot green chillies,
sliced into fine rounds

½ teaspoon ground turmeric

2 teaspoons ground cumin

½ fresh coconut, finely grated (page 18)

½ teaspoon salt

Wash and scrub the mussels well, removing the beards that are often attached
to them. Discard any shells that are open.

Put the ginger and garlic into the container of an electric blender or food
processor. Add 120 ml (4 fl oz) water and blend until fairly smooth.

Put the oil in a large pan and set over medium heat. When hot, put in the
onions and sauté them until they turn translucent. Now put in the paste from the
blender, green chillies, turmeric and cumin. Stir and fry for a minute. Add the
coconut, salt and 250 ml (8 fl oz) water. Bring to a boil. (This much of the recipe
may be made several hours ahead of time.) Add the mussels. Mix well and bring
to a boil. Cover tightly. Lower heat slightly and let the mussels steam for
6–10 minutes or until they open up. Discard any mussels that fail to open. Serve
immediately.

prawns with courgettes

Jhinga aur ghia

We do not have courgettes in India but we do have a variety of similar squashes which are often cooked with prawns and other seafood. Here is one such combination.

I prefer to use relatively small courgettes weighing about 100 g (4 oz) each. If you can only get larger ones, just cut them appropriately so that each piece is just a little larger than a prawn.

I like to serve these prawns with Spiced Basmati Rice (page 194) or Plain Long-grain Rice (page 192) and Red Split Lentils with Cumin Seeds (page 165).

Serves 4

350 g (12 oz) courgettes (see above)

1¼ teaspoons salt

350 g (12 oz) peeled, good-quality frozen prawns, defrosted and patted dry

5 tablespoons vegetable oil

6 cloves garlic, peeled and very finely chopped

75 g (3 oz) finely chopped, fresh green coriander (weight without lower stems and roots)

1 fresh, hot green chilli, finely chopped

½ teaspoon ground turmeric

1½ teaspoons ground cumin

¼ teaspoon cayenne pepper

3 small canned tomatoes, finely chopped, plus 120 ml (4 fl oz) liquid from can

1 teaspoon peeled, very finely grated fresh ginger

1 tablespoon lemon juice

Scrub the courgettes and trim them. Now cut them in 4 slices lengthwise. Cut each slice, lengthwise, into 4 long strips. Cut the strips into thirds, crosswise. Put the courgettes in a bowl. Sprinkle ¼ teaspoon of the salt over the pieces. Toss to mix and set aside for 30–40 minutes. Drain and pat dry.

Put the prawns on kitchen paper and dry them off as well.

Put the oil in a wide pan or frying-pan and set over medium-high heat. When hot, put in the chopped garlic. Stir and fry until the garlic pieces turn a medium-brown colour. Put in the courgettes, fresh coriander, green chilli, turmeric, cumin, cayenne, tomatoes and their liquid, ginger, lemon juice and remaining 1 teaspoon salt. Stir to mix and bring to a simmer. Add the prawns and stir them in. Cover, turn heat to low and simmer for 3 minutes.

Uncover, turn the heat to medium and boil away the liquid, if there is any, so that you are left with a thick sauce.

prawns in a dark sauce

Rasedar jhinga

Serve this with Plain Basmati Rice (page 193), Cauliflower with Potatoes (page 144), and Tomato, Onion and Green Coriander Relish (page 215).

Serves 4

75 g (3 oz) onions, peeled and coarsely chopped

5 cloves garlic, peeled

2.5 cm (1 inch) cube fresh ginger, peeled and coarsely chopped

3 tablespoons plus 300 ml (10 fl oz) water

4 tablespoons vegetable oil

2.5 cm (1 inch) cinnamon stick

6 cardamom pods

2 bay leaves

2 teaspoons ground cumin

1 teaspoon ground coriander

175 g (6 oz) tomatoes, peeled (page 30) and very finely chopped

5 tablespoons natural yoghurt

1/2 teaspoon ground turmeric

1/4 –1/2 teaspoon cayenne pepper

About 3/4 teaspoon salt

350 g (12 oz) peeled, good-quality frozen prawns, defrosted and patted dry

1/4 teaspoon *garam masala* (page 21)

2 tablespoons finely chopped, fresh green coriander

Blend the onions, garlic, ginger and 3 tablespoons water in an electric blender until you have a paste.

Put the oil in a 20–23 cm (8–9 inch) wide pan and set over medium-high heat. When hot, put in the cinnamon, cardamom pods and bay leaves. Stir for 3–4 seconds. Put in the paste from the blender. Stir and fry for about 5 minutes or until the paste turns a light brown colour. Add the cumin and ground coriander. Stir and fry for 30 seconds. Put in the tomatoes. Stir and keep frying until the paste has a nice reddish-brown look to it. Now put in 1 tablespoon of the yoghurt. Stir and fry for 10–15 seconds or until it is incorporated in the sauce. Add all the yoghurt this way. Add the turmeric and cayenne and stir for a minute. Put in 300 ml (10 fl oz) water, the salt and the prawns. Stir to mix and bring to a boil over medium-high heat. Stir and cook for about 5 minutes or until you have a thick sauce. Do not overcook. Sprinkle with the *garam masala* and mix. Garnish with fresh coriander.

halibut with cauliflower

Macchi aur phool gobi

All you need to serve with this dish is some rice and a relish.

Serves 4 to 6

2.5 cm (1 inch) thick halibut steak, weighing about 900 g (2 lb); 2 smaller steaks of equal thickness will do

1½ teaspoons ground cumin

1½ teaspoons ground coriander

½ teaspoon ground turmeric

About ½ teaspoon cayenne pepper

1½ teaspoons salt

100 g (4 oz) onions, peeled and coarsely chopped

Two 2.5 cm (1 inch) cubes fresh ginger, peeled and coarsely chopped

1–2 fresh, hot green chillies, roughly cut into 3–4 pieces each

3 tablespoons plus 450 ml (15 fl oz) water

7 tablespoons vegetable oil

350 g (12 oz) florets from a cauliflower head, each about 5 cm (2 inches) in length and about 2.5 cm (1 inch) across at the top

Freshly ground black pepper

6 tablespoons natural yoghurt

Have the fishmonger cut the halibut steak into pieces approximately 5 x 4 x 2.5 cm (2 x 1½ x 1 inches). Or do this at home with a heavy cleaver that can hack through the bone. Leave the skin on.

Put the fish pieces in a bowl. Sprinkle ½ teaspoon of the cumin, ½ teaspoon of the coriander, ¼ teaspoon of the turmeric, ¼ teaspoon of the cayenne and ½ teaspoon of the salt over them. Toss to mix evenly. Set aside for ½–1 hour.

Put the onions, ginger, green chillies and 3 tablespoons water into the container of an electric blender. Blend until you have a paste.

Heat 6 tablespoons of the oil in a 30 cm (12 inch), preferably non-stick, sauté pan or deep frying-pan over medium heat. When hot, put in the cauliflower florets. Stir and fry them until they are very lightly browned. Remove with a slotted spoon and set aside in a bowl. Sprinkle ¼ teaspoon of the salt and some black pepper over the cauliflower. Toss to mix.

Put the fish pieces into the same pan in a single layer and brown lightly on both sides. Do not let the fish cook through. Remove the fish pieces carefully and put on a plate.

Add another tablespoon of oil to the pan and set over medium-high heat. When hot, put in the paste from the blender. Stir and fry the paste until it turns a light brown colour. Now add the remaining 1 teaspoon cumin, 1 teaspoon coriander, ⅛–¼ teaspoon cayenne and ¾ teaspoon salt. Stir and fry for a minute. Put in 1 tablespoon of the yoghurt. Stir and fry it for about 30 seconds or until it is incorporated into the paste. Add all the yoghurt this way, 1 tablespoon at a time. Now pour in 450 ml (15 fl oz) water, stir and bring to a simmer. Simmer on medium heat for 2 minutes. Gently put in the fish pieces and the cauliflower. Cover partially and cook on medium heat for about 5 minutes or until the fish is cooked through and the cauliflower is tender, spooning the sauce over the fish and vegetables several times.

fried plaice fillets

Tali hui macchi

This is one of the simpler fish dishes served in many parts of India, with each area using its own local fish. The breading is, of course, a Western influence. Wedges of lemon or some tomato ketchup may be served on the side.

Serves 4

700 g (1½ lb) plaice fillets with dark skin removed

¾ teaspoon salt

Freshly ground black pepper

1½ teaspoons ground cumin

½ teaspoon ground turmeric

½ teaspoon cayenne pepper

2 tablespoons very finely chopped, fresh green coriander (parsley may be substituted)

2 large eggs

4 teaspoons water

175 g (6 oz) fresh breadcrumbs

Vegetable oil for shallow-frying (enough to have 1 cm/½ inch in frying-pan)

Cut the fish fillets, crosswise and at a slight diagonal, into 2 cm (¾ inch) wide strips. Lay the strips on a plate and sprinkle both sides with the salt, black pepper, cumin, turmeric, cayenne and fresh coriander or parsley. Pat down the spices. Set aside for 15 minutes.

Break the eggs into a deep plate. Add 4 teaspoons water and beat lightly. Spread the breadcrumbs on a plate. Dip the fish in the egg and then in the crumbs to coat evenly.

Put about 1 cm (½ inch) oil in a large frying-pan and set over a medium heat. When hot, put in as many pieces of fish as the pan will hold easily. Fry for 2–3 minutes on each side or until golden-brown. Drain on kitchen paper. Fry all the fish strips this way and serve hot.

cod steaks in a spicy tomato sauce

Timatar wali macchi

I like to serve this with Rice and Peas (page 196) and Spinach Cooked with Onions (page 156).

Serves 4

4 cod steaks, weighing about 900 g (2 lb)

1¼ teaspoons salt

½ teaspoon cayenne pepper

¼ teaspoon ground turmeric

9 tablespoons vegetable oil

1 teaspoon fennel seeds

1 teaspoon mustard seeds

175 g (6 oz) onions, peeled and finely chopped

2 cloves garlic, peeled and finely chopped

2 teaspoons ground cumin

One 400 g (14 oz) can of tomatoes, with the tomatoes chopped up

½ teaspoon ground, roasted cumin seeds (page 20), optional

¼ teaspoon *garam masala* (page 21)

Pat the fish steaks dry with kitchen paper. Rub them, on both sides, with ¼ teaspoon of the salt, ¼ teaspoon of the cayenne and the turmeric. Set aside for 30 minutes.

Put 4 tablespoons of the oil in a saucepan and set over medium heat. When hot, put in the fennel and mustard seeds. As soon as the mustard seeds begin to pop – this just takes a few seconds – put in the onions and garlic. Stir and fry until the onions turn slightly brown. Now put in the cumin, 1 teaspoon salt and ¼ teaspoon cayenne. Stir once and put in the tomatoes and their liquid, the ground, roasted cumin seeds, if using, and the *garam masala*. Bring to a boil. Cover, turn heat to low, and simmer gently for 15 minutes.

Meanwhile, **pre-heat** the oven to 180°C/350°F/Gas 4.

Put the remaining 5 tablespoons of the oil in a large, preferably non-stick, frying-pan and set over medium-high heat. When hot, put in the fish steaks and brown on both sides. Do not cook the fish through. Put the steaks in a baking dish. Pour the cooked tomato sauce over the fish and bake, uncovered, for 15 minutes or until the fish is done.

grilled mackerel with lemon and fresh coriander

Hare masale mali macchi

Indian mackerel seem to me to be much plumper than their English counterparts. Perhaps the warmer waters make them lazier. Goan fishermen on India's west coast roast them right on the beach over smouldering rice straws. The blackened skin is then peeled away and the now pristine, skinless fish served with a simple vinegar dressing. A good fresh mackerel needs nothing more.

Further up the same coast, in large cities like Bombay, the fish is marinated first in a dressing of lemon juice and fresh green coriander and then fried or grilled. Here is the Bombay recipe. I often serve it with Mushroom *Pullao* (page 199) and Cabbage with Peas (page 140).

Serves 2

2 medium-sized, whole mackerel, about 750 g (1½ lb) in all, cleaned

3 tablespoons very finely chopped, fresh green coriander

½–1 fresh, hot green chilli, finely chopped

1 tablespoon lemon juice

½ teaspoon salt

Freshly ground black pepper

50 g (2 oz) unsalted butter, cut into pats

Cut the heads off the mackerel. Split them all the way down the stomach and then lay them out flat, skinside up, on a firm surface.

Now bone the fish this way: Press down firmly with the heel of your hand all along the backbone. This should loosen the bone from the flesh somewhat. Now turn the fish over so the skinside is down. Work your fingers (or else use a knife) under the bones to prise them away from the fish.

Cut 2–3 shallow diagonal slashes on the skinside of each fish.

Combine the fresh coriander, green chilli, lemon juice, salt and black pepper in a bowl. Mix well. Rub this mixture all over the fish. Set aside for 45 minutes.

Heat the grill. Put the fish in the grill pan, with the rack removed, skinside up, and dot with half the butter. Grill, 10 cm (4 inches) away from the heat, for about 5 minutes. Turn the fish over, dot with the remaining butter and grill for 4 minutes or until golden-brown.

love all vegetables — from shiny purple aubergines that can be fried very simply with a light dusting of turmeric and cayenne to the humble potato which, in India, is cooked in at least a thousand different ways including one in which black pepper is the main seasoning.

As many Indians are vegetarians, we have, over the years, worked out a great variety of ways to cook our everyday vegetables such as cabbages, green beans, beetroots and carrots. Sometimes the vegetables are cut into shreds or slices and quickly stir-fried with whole spices such as cumin seeds and mustard seeds. These are referred to as 'dry' vegetables and rarely have even the glimmer of a sauce. At other times we may cook root vegetables in a thick ginger-garlic sauce or with tomatoes. Such dishes are referred to as 'wet' dishes because of the sauce. They are generally served in small, individual bowls. Both 'dry' and 'wet' dishes may be served with rice or Indian breads.

For those of you who are vegetarians — or want to cut down on your meat intake — you can make perfectly balanced meals by picking two or three vegetables from this chapter and then adding a pulse dish, a rice or bread and a yoghurt relish.

vegetables

gujerati-style green beans

Gujerati sem

Here is a very simple, yet delicious way to cook green beans. This dish goes well both with Indian meals and with grilled and roast meats (I like it with sausages). Gujeratis often cook green vegetables with a little baking soda in order to preserve their bright colour. I am told that this kills the vitamins. So I blanch the beans and rinse them out quickly under cold, running water instead. This works equally well. I generally do the blanching and rinsing ahead of time and do the final cooking just before we sit down to eat.

If you do not want the beans to be hot, either do without the red chilli or else discard all its seeds and use just the skin for flavour.

Serves 4

450 g (1 lb) fresh green French beans
4 tablespoons vegetable oil
1 tablespoon black mustard seeds
4 cloves garlic, peeled and very finely chopped
1/2–1 hot, dried red chilli, coarsely crushed in a mortar
1 teaspoon salt
1/2 teaspoon sugar
Freshly ground black pepper

Trim the beans and cut them into 2.5 cm (1 inch) lengths. Blanch the beans by dropping them into a pan of boiling water and boiling rapidly for 3–4 minutes or until they are just tender. Drain immediately in a colander and rinse under cold, running water. Set aside.

Put the oil in a large frying-pan and set over medium heat. When hot, put in the mustard seeds. As soon as the mustard seeds begin to pop, put in the garlic. Stir the garlic pieces around until they turn light brown. Put in the crushed red chilli and stir for a few seconds. Put in the green beans, salt and sugar. Stir to mix. Turn the heat to medium-low. Stir and cook the beans for 7–8 minutes or until they have absorbed the flavour of the spices. Add the black pepper, mix and serve.

spicy green beans

Masaledar sem

These green beans may, of course, be served with an Indian dinner. But they could perk up a simple meal of roast chicken, pork chops or meat loaf as well. They are tart and hot and would complement the plainest of everyday foods with their zesty blend of flavours. Another good thing about them – they may be made ahead of time and reheated.

Serves 6

750 g (1½ lb) fresh green French beans

Piece fresh ginger, about 4 cm (1½ inches) long and 2.5 cm (1 inch) thick, peeled and coarsely chopped

10 cloves garlic, peeled

350 ml (12 fl oz) water

5 tablespoons vegetable oil

2 teaspoons cumin seeds

1 dried, hot red chilli, lightly crushed in a mortar

2 teaspoons ground coriander

225g (8 oz) tomatoes, peeled (page 30) and finely chopped

About 1¼ teaspoons salt

3 tablespoons lemon juice, or to taste

1 teaspoon ground, roasted cumin seeds (page 20)

Freshly ground black pepper

Trim the green beans and cut them, crosswise, at 5 mm (¼ inch) intervals. Put the ginger and garlic into the container of an electric blender or food processor. Add 120 ml (4 fl oz) of the measured water and blend until fairly smooth.

Put the oil in a wide, heavy pan and set over medium heat. When hot, put in the cumin seeds. Five seconds later, put in the crushed chilli. As soon as it darkens, pour in the ginger-garlic paste. Stir and cook for about a minute. Put in the coriander. Stir a few times. Now put in the chopped tomatoes. Stir and cook for about 2 minutes, mashing up the tomato pieces with the back of a slotted spoon as you do so. Put in the beans, salt and the remaining water. Bring to a simmer. Cover, turn heat to low and cook for 8–10 minutes or until the beans are tender. Remove the cover. Add the lemon juice, ground, roasted cumin seeds and a generous amount of freshly ground black pepper.

Turn heat up and boil away all of the liquid, stirring the beans gently as you do so.

green beans with ginger and green coriander

Hare masale ki sem

You may serve these tangy, ginger- and green-coriander-flavoured green beans
with almost any Indian meal or with roast leg of lamb, roast chicken or even sausages.
Cold left-overs may be tossed into a green salad.
The green beans should, ideally, be cut crosswise into 5 mm (¼ inch) segments.
However, if you are feeling lazy as I often do, you may cut them into 1 cm (½ inch) or
2.5 cm (1 inch) lengths. Just cut them evenly, whatever length you choose.

Serves 4 to 5

550 g (1¼ lb) fresh green beans

2.5 cm (1 inch) piece fresh ginger, peeled and very thinly sliced

4 tablespoons vegetable oil

½ teaspoon black mustard seeds

2 teaspoons ground cumin

¼ teaspoon ground turmeric

¾ teaspoon salt, or to taste

1 fresh, hot green chilli, finely chopped

4 teaspoons lemon juice

150 ml (5 fl oz) chicken stock or water

5–6 tablespoons finely chopped, fresh green coriander

Trim the green beans and cut them, crosswise, into 2.5 cm (1 inch) segments (see above).

Stack a few ginger slices together at a time and cut them into very fine strips.

Put the oil in a large frying-pan or wok and set over medium high heat. When hot, put in the mustard seeds. As soon as the mustard seeds begin to pop – this takes just a few seconds – put in the ginger strips. Stir and fry until the ginger starts to brown, a matter of a few seconds. Put in the green beans and toss once or twice. Now put in the cumin, turmeric, salt and green chilli. Toss once or twice. Add the lemon juice and chicken stock or water. Stir and bring to a simmer. Cover, turn heat to low and simmer gently for 10 minutes or until the beans are almost tender. Add the fresh coriander, toss and cover again for a minute. Uncover, toss and boil away all liquid (if any is left) at a higher heat.

fried aubergine slices

Tala hua baigan

This is one of the simplest ways of cooking aubergines in India. Ideally, the frying should be done at the very last minute and the melt-in-the-mouth slices served as soon as they come out of the hot oil. Sometimes I arrange these slices, like petals, around a roast leg of lamb. They can, of course, be served with any Indian meal.

Left-over aubergine slices, if there are any, may be heated together with any left-over, Indian-style meat the following day. The combination makes for a very good new dish.

Serves 4 to 6

550 g (1¼ lb) aubergine
About 1 teaspoon salt
½ teaspoon ground turmeric
⅛ – ½ teaspoon cayenne pepper
Some freshly ground black pepper
Vegetable oil for shallow-frying
6–8 lemon wedges

Cut the aubergine into quarters, lengthwise, and then cut, crosswise, into 1 cm (½ inch) thick wedges.

Mix the salt, turmeric, cayenne and black pepper in a small bowl. Sprinkle this combination over the aubergine wedges and mix well.

Put about 1 cm (⅓ inch) oil in a 20–23 cm (8–9 inch) frying-pan and set over medium heat. When hot, put in as many aubergine slices as the pan will hold in a single layer. Fry until reddish-gold on one side. Turn the slices and fry them on their second side. Remove with a slotted spoon and spread out on a plate lined with kitchen paper.

Do a second batch, adding more oil, if you need to.

Serve with lemon wedges.

beetroot with onions

Shorvedar chukander

I love beetroot, in almost any form. Even people who do not have a weakness for this particular root vegetable, manage to succumb to the charms of this recipe. It is a kind of stew, thickened by the onions floating around in it and somewhat tart in flavour because of the tomatoes it contains. As there is a fair amount of sauce, I frequently serve it with Beef Baked with Yoghurt and Black Pepper (page 69), a somewhat dry dish, and with Tomato, Onion and Green Coriander Relish (page 215). *Chapatis* are the ideal bread to serve with this meal, though plain rice would also taste good.

Serves 3 to 4

350 g (12 oz) raw beetroot
(weight without stems and leaves)

4 tablespoons vegetable oil

1 teaspoon cumin seeds

1 clove garlic, peeled and
very finely chopped

100 g (4 oz) onions, peeled and
coarsely chopped

1 teaspoon plain flour

$^{1}/_{8}-^{1}/_{2}$ teaspoon cayenne pepper

225 g (8 oz) tomatoes, peeled (page 30)
and very finely chopped

1 teaspoon salt

300 ml (10 fl oz) water

Peel the beetroot and cut them into wedges. A medium-sized beetroot, about 5 cm (2 inches) in length, should, for example, be cut into 6 wedges.

Put the oil in a medium-sized pan and set over medium heat. When hot, put in the cumin seeds. Let them sizzle for 5 seconds. Put in the garlic. Stir and fry until the garlic pieces turn golden. Put in the onions. Stir and fry for 2 minutes. Put in the flour and cayenne. Stir and fry for a minute. Now put in the beetroot, the tomatoes, salt and water. Bring to a simmer. Cover, turn heat to low and simmer for 30 minutes or until the beetroot are tender. Remove lid, turn up heat to medium, and cook uncovered for about 7 minutes or until the sauce has thickened slightly.

This dish may be made ahead of time and reheated.

cauliflower with onion and tomato

Phool gobi ki bhaji

A good all-round vegetable dish that goes well with most Indian meat dishes.

Serves 6

Two medium-sized cauliflowers, about 1 kg (2¼ lb) in all (you need about 725 g/1 lb 10 oz florets)

75 g (3 oz) onions, peeled and coarsely chopped

Two 2.5 cm (1 inch) cubes fresh ginger, peeled and coarsely chopped

About 7 tablespoons water

5 tablespoons vegetable oil

6 cloves garlic, peeled and very finely chopped

1 teaspoon ground cumin

1 teaspoon ground coriander

150–175 g (5–6 oz) tomatoes, peeled (page 30) and finely chopped

½ teaspoon ground turmeric

¼ –½ teaspoon cayenne pepper

½ –1 fresh, hot green chilli, finely chopped

1 tablespoon lemon juice

1¾ teaspoons salt

¼ teaspoon *garam masala* (page 21)

Break up the cauliflowers into florets that are about 4 cm (1½ inches) across at the head and 4–5 cm (1½ –2 inches) in length.

Let them soak in a bowl of water for 30 minutes. Drain.

Put the onions and ginger into the container of an electric blender along with 4 tablespoons of the water. Blend until you have a paste.

Put the oil in a 23–25 cm (9–10 inch) wide pan or deep frying-pan and set over medium-high heat. When hot, put in the garlic. Stir and fry until the pieces turn a medium-brown colour. Put in the cauliflower. Stir and fry for about 2 minutes or until the cauliflower pieces pick up a few brown spots. Remove the cauliflower with a slotted spoon and put in a bowl. Put the onion-ginger mixture into the same pan. Stir and fry it for a minute. Now put in the cumin, coriander and tomatoes. Stir and fry this mixture until it turns a medium-brown colour. If it starts to catch, turn the heat down slightly and sprinkle in a tablespoon of water. Then keep frying until you have the right colour. Add the turmeric, cayenne, green chilli, lemon juice and salt. Give a few good stirs and turn heat to low. Now put in the cauliflower and any possible liquid in the cauliflower bowl. Stir gently to mix. Add 3 tablespoons of the water, stir again and bring to a simmer. Cover and cook on gentle heat, stirring now and then, for 5–10 minutes or until the cauliflower is just done. Remove lid and sprinkle *garam masala* over the top. Stir to mix.

cauliflower with potatoes

Phool gobi aur aloo ki bhaji

This is the kind of comforting 'homey' dish that most North Indians enjoy. It has no sauce and is generally eaten with a bread. I like to serve 'Royal' Lamb or Beef with a Creamy Almond Sauce (page 80) or Tandoori-style Chicken (page 90) with it.

Serves 4 to 6

225 g (8 oz) potatoes

1 medium-sized cauliflower (you need 450 g/1 lb florets)

5 tablespoons vegetable oil

1 teaspoon cumin seeds

1 teaspoon ground cumin

1/2 teaspoon ground coriander

1/4 teaspoon ground turmeric

1/4 teaspoon cayenne pepper

1/2 –1 fresh, hot green chilli, very finely chopped

1/2 teaspoon ground, roasted cumin seeds (page 20)

1 teaspoon salt

Freshly ground black pepper

Boil the potatoes in their jackets and allow them to cool completely. (Day-old cooked potatoes that have been refrigerated work very well for this dish.) Peel the potatoes and cut them into 2 cm (3/4 inch) dice.

Break up the cauliflower into chunky florets that are about 4 cm (1½ inches) across at the head and about 4 cm (1½ inches) long. Soak the florets in a bowl of water for 30 minutes. Drain.

Put the oil in a large, preferably non-stick, frying-pan and set over medium heat. When hot, put in the cumin seeds. Let the seeds sizzle for 3–4 seconds. Now put in the cauliflower and stir it about for 2 minutes. Let the cauliflower brown in spots. Cover, turn heat to low and simmer for about 4–6 minutes or until the cauliflower is almost done but still has a hint of crispness left. Put in the diced potatoes, ground cumin, coriander, turmeric, cayenne, green chilli, ground, roasted cumin seeds, salt and some black pepper. Stir gently to mix. Continue to cook uncovered on low heat for another 3 minutes or until the potatoes are heated through.

Stir gently as you do so.

cauliflower with cumin and asafetida

Heeng zeere ki gobi

This simple, everyday dish may also be made with broccoli. Even though the broccoli will lose some of its bright green colour, it will still taste very good.

Serves 4

550 g (1¼ lb) head cauliflower

3 tablespoons vegetable oil

Generous pinch of ground asafetida

½ teaspoon cumin seeds

85 g (3 oz) onions, peeled and cut into very fine half-rings

½–1 fresh, hot green chilli, finely chopped

1 teaspoon ground cumin

½ teaspoon ground coriander

¼ teaspoon ground turmeric

⅛–¼ teaspoon cayenne pepper, or to taste

¾ teaspoon salt, or to taste

120 ml (4 fl oz) water

2 teaspoons lemon juice

Break the cauliflower into florets that are about 4 cm (1½ inches) across at the head and 4–5 cm (1½–2 inches) in length. The stem may be peeled and cut into 5 mm (¼ inch) rounds.

Put the oil in a large frying-pan or wok and set over medium-high heat. When hot, put in the asafetida. A second later, put in the cumin seeds. Wait about 10 seconds and add the onions. Stir and fry for about 2 minutes or until the onion slices brown. Now put in the cauliflower and green chilli. Turn heat down to medium and toss. Add the ground cumin, ground coriander, turmeric, cayenne and salt. Toss for another minute. Add the water and lemon juice, toss and bring to a simmer. Cover, turn heat to low and cook for 5–7 minutes or until the cauliflower is just tender.

cauliflower with fennel and mustard seeds

Baghari phool gobi

You could serve this dish with Chicken in a Red Sweet Pepper Sauce (page 101) and rice.

Serves 6

1 large or 2 medium-sized cauliflowers (you need about 900 g/2 lb florets)

7 tablespoons vegetable oil

2 teaspoons fennel seeds

1 tablespoon black mustard seeds

1 tablespoon peeled, very finely chopped garlic

¼ teaspoon ground turmeric

¼–⅓ teaspoon cayenne pepper

About 1½ teaspoons salt

About 4 tablespoons water

Cut the cauliflower into delicate florets that are no longer than 5 cm (2 inches), no wider at the head than 2.5 cm (1 inch) and about 1 cm (⅓ inch) thick. Put them into a bowl of water for at least 30 minutes. Drain them just before you get ready to cook.

Put the oil in a large, 25–30 cm (10–12 inch) frying-pan and set over medium heat. When hot, put in the fennel and mustard seeds. As soon as the mustard seeds begin to pop, put in the finely chopped garlic. Stir and fry until the garlic pieces are lightly browned. Add the turmeric and cayenne. Stir once and quickly put in the cauliflower, salt and water. Stir and cook on medium heat for 6–7 minutes or until the cauliflower is just done. It should retain its crispness and there should be no liquid left. If the water evaporates before the cauliflower is done, add a little more.

(If your frying-pan is smaller than the suggested size, the cauliflower will take longer to cook. In that case, it might be a good idea to cover it for 5 minutes.)

carrots, peas and potatoes flavoured with cumin

Gajar, matar, aur aloo ki bhaji

Here is a simple, quick-cooking dish. Ideally, it should be made in an Indian *karhai* but if you do not have one, a large frying-pan or sauté pan will do. The vegetables are cooked in a Bengali style but could easily accompany a roast chicken or grilled sausages.

Serves 6

175 g (6 oz) carrots

175 g (6 oz) potatoes, boiled, drained and cooled

175 g (6 oz) onions

1 spring onion

3 tablespoons mustard oil (another vegetable oil may be substituted)

1½ teaspoons cumin seeds

2 dried, hot red chillies

175 g (6 oz) shelled peas

About 1 teaspoon salt

¼ teaspoon sugar

Peel the carrots and cut them first into 1 cm (½ inch) thick diagonal slices and then into 1 cm (½ inch) dice.

Peel the potatoes and cut them into 1 cm (½ inch) dice. Peel the onions and chop them coarsely. Cut the spring onion into very, very thin slices, all the way to the end of its green section.

Put the oil in a large frying-pan and set over medium heat. When hot, put in the cumin seeds. Let them sizzle for 3–4 seconds. Now put in the chillies and stir them about for 3–4 seconds. Put in the chopped onions. Stir and cook for 5 minutes or until the onion pieces turn translucent. Put in the carrots and peas. Stir them about for a minute. Cover, turn heat to low, and cook for about 5 minutes or until the vegetables are tender. Uncover and turn heat up slightly. Add the potatoes, salt and sugar. Stir and cook another 2–3 minutes. Add the spring onion. Stir and cook for 30 seconds.

Note: Remove the whole chillies before serving.

Pulses — dried beans, split peas and lentils — are a staple in India and help provide a large measure of the daily protein for families who eat meat rarely or are vegetarian. But pulses, by themselves, are an incomplete food and need to be complemented — at the same meal — with a grain (rice or bread) and a dairy product (such as yoghurt or cheese). When nutritionists tell us today that this food combination has as much protein as a steak, I cannot help but think of the villagers in India whose basic diet, for centuries, has been *dals* (split peas) and rice or bread, washed down with a glass of buttermilk. Perhaps these villagers are not so badly off, after all!

Apart from their food value, I find pulses very versatile. Their non-assertive taste and textures allow them to be used easily in soups. They also combine beautifully with meats and vegetables to make excellent main courses.

Sometimes pulses can be hard to digest. The same Indian forebears who worked out that a nutritionally balanced vegetarian meal contained pulses, grains and dairy products, also knew — I do not know how — that certain seasonings made pulses more digestible. Today pulses in India are almost always cooked with at least one of the following: ginger, asafetida and turmeric.

We have many different types of pulses in India. Some are left whole, others are split and sometimes skinned. It is the split ones that are called *dals*. The splitting helps to cook them much faster.

All pulses need to be picked over and washed, as the packets often include small stones and husks. Whole beans should either be soaked in water overnight before they are cooked or else they can be boiled in water for 2 minutes and then left to soak in the boiling water for an hour. The cooking time for all pulses varies according to their freshness. The fresher they are, the faster they cook. When cooking split peas, Indians always leave the lid slightly ajar. The reason for this is that split peas create a lot of thick froth as they cook and this blocks up the normal escape routes for the steam. So the pot boils over, creating a mess on the cooker. Leaving the lid slightly ajar helps to avoid this.

All beans should be stored in tightly lidded containers. Overleaf there is a description of the pulses I have used in this book.

pulses

Red split lentils Masoor dal These salmon-coloured, round, split lentils are available widely in most supermarkets. They turn pale yellow during cooking and have a pleasant, mild flavour.

Whole green lentils These round, flying-saucer-shaped, greenish-brown lentils are very similar to our unsplit, unskinned *masoor*. They are available in all supermarkets and have the virtue of cooking quite fast.

Moong dal This is the skinned and split version of the same mung bean that is used to make bean sprouts for oriental cooking. The grains are pale yellow and somewhat elongated. This is, perhaps, the most popular North Indian *dal*. It has a mild, aristocratic flavour and is sold by Indian, Pakistani and Greek grocers, and increasingly by many supermarkets.

Chana dal This is very similar to the yellow split peas that are sold in supermarkets, only the grains are smaller and the flavour 'meatier' and sweeter. *Chana dal* is sold mainly by Indian and Pakistani grocers. Yellow split peas may be substituted for *chana dal* in my recipes.

Black-eyed beans Lobhia These excellent beans, greyish or beige ovals, graced with a dark dot, are sold widely in all supermarkets. They have a slightly smokey flavour.

Chick peas Chhole This large, heart-shaped, beige-coloured pea is sold by most supermarkets as well as South Asian and Middle Eastern grocers. It lends itself to being cooked as a spicy snack food as well as being combined with meats and vegetables.

Red kidney beans Rajma These large, dark red, kidney-shaped beans are available in all supermarkets as well as Asian grocers.

Aduki beans Ma These smaller red beans look like the children of red kidney beans. For some reason, they are sold by their Japanese name, *aduki*.

red split lentils with cumin seeds

Masoor dal

This salmon-coloured split pea turns dull yellow when cooked. It is sold as 'Egyptian lentils' in some Middle Eastern stores. It is best served with a rice dish and almost any Indian meat and vegetable you like.

Serves 4 to 6

200 g (7 oz) red split lentils (*masoor dal*), picked over, washed and drained

1 litre (1³/₄ pints) water

2 thin slices unpeeled ginger

¹/₂ teaspoon ground turmeric

1 teaspoon salt, or to taste

3 tablespoons *ghee* (page 28) or vegetable oil

Pinch of ground asafetida (optional)

1 teaspoon cumin seeds

1 teaspoon ground coriander

¹/₄ teaspoon cayenne pepper

2 tablespoons finely chopped, fresh green coriander

Combine the lentils and water in a heavy pan. Bring to a simmer. Remove any scum that collects at the top. Add the ginger and turmeric. Stir to mix. Cover, leaving the lid very slightly ajar, turn heat to low and simmer gently for 1¹/₂ hours or until the lentils are tender. Stir every 5 minutes during the last 30 minutes to prevent sticking. Add the salt and stir to mix. Remove ginger slices.

Put the *ghee* or oil in a small frying-pan and set over medium heat. When hot, put in the asafetida, if using. A second later, put in the cumin seeds. Let the seeds sizzle for a few seconds. Now put in the ground coriander and cayenne. Stir once and then quickly pour the contents of the frying-pan – the *ghee* and spices – into the pan with the lentils. Stir to mix.

Sprinkle the fresh coriander over the top when you serve.

moong dal and red lentils with browned onion

Mili moong aur masoor dal

Here two pulses are combined in an earthy, wholesome and utterly delicious preparation, one that I eat at least once or twice a week. I like to serve it with Plain Basmati Rice (page 193) and any meat or vegetable dish.

Serves 6 to 8

175 g (6 oz) *moong dal*

175 g (6 oz) red split lentils (*masoor dal*)

1.2 litres (2 pints) water

$\frac{1}{2}$ teaspoon ground turmeric

$1\frac{1}{4}$ –$1\frac{1}{2}$ teaspoons salt

4 tablespoons vegetable oil or *ghee* (page 28)

Generous pinch of ground asafetida

1 teaspoon cumin seeds

3–5 dried, hot red chillies

1 small onion, peeled and cut into very thin half-rings

Pick over the *moong dal* and red lentils. Combine them in a bowl and wash in several changes of water. Drain. Put in a heavy pan. Add the water and turmeric. Stir and bring to a simmer. (Do not let it boil over.) Cover in such a way as to leave the lid just very slightly ajar, turn heat to low and simmer gently for 40–50 minutes or until the pulses are tender. Stir a few times during the cooking. Add the salt and mix. Leave covered, on very low heat, as you do the next step.

Put the oil or *ghee* in a small frying-pan and set over high heat. When hot, put in the asafetida, then, a second later, the cumin seeds. Let the cumin seeds sizzle for a few seconds. Put in the red chillies. As soon as they turn dark red (this takes just a few seconds), put in the onion. Stir and fry on medium-high heat until the onion turns quite brown and crisp. You may need to turn the heat down a bit towards the end to prevent burning. Now lift up the lid of the *dal* pan and pour in the contents of the frying-pan, oil as well as spices and onion.

Cover the pan immediately to trap the aromas.

black-eyed beans with mushrooms

Lohbia aur khumbi

I like this bean dish so much I often find myself eating it up with a spoon, all by itself. At a meal, I serve it with Red Lamb or Beef Stew (page 70) or with Chicken in a Fried Onion Sauce (page 93). Rice or Indian breads should be served on the side.

Serves 6

225 g (8 oz) dried black-eyed beans, picked over, washed and drained

1.2 litres (2 pints) water

225 g (8 oz) fresh mushrooms

6 tablespoons vegetable oil

1 teaspoon cumin seeds

2.5 cm (1 inch) cinnamon stick

150 g (5 oz) onions, peeled and chopped

4 cloves garlic, peeled and very finely chopped

400 g (14 oz) tomatoes, peeled (page 30) and chopped

2 teaspoons ground coriander

1 teaspoon ground cumin

½ teaspoon ground turmeric

¼ teaspoon cayenne pepper

2 teaspoons salt

Freshly ground black pepper

3 tablespoons chopped, fresh green coriander (fresh parsley may be substituted)

Put the beans and water into a heavy pan and bring to a boil. Cover, turn heat to low and simmer gently for 2 minutes. Turn off the heat and let the pan sit, covered and undisturbed, for 1 hour.

While the pan is resting, cut the mushrooms through their stems into 3 mm (⅛ inch) thick slices.

Put the oil in a frying-pan and set over medium-high heat. When hot, put in the cumin seeds and the cinnamon stick. Let them sizzle for 5–6 seconds. Now put in the onions and garlic. Stir and fry until the onion pieces turn brown at the edges. Put in the mushrooms. Stir and fry until the mushrooms wilt. Now put in the tomatoes, ground coriander, cumin, turmeric and cayenne. Stir and cook for a minute. Cover, turn heat to low and let this mixture cook in its own juices for 10 minutes. Turn off the heat under the frying-pan.

Bring the beans to a boil again. Cover, turn heat to low and simmer for 20–30 minutes or until the beans are tender. To this bean and water mixture, add the mushroom mixture, salt, black pepper and fresh coriander or parsley. Stir to mix and bring to a simmer. Simmer, uncovered, on medium-low heat for another 30 minutes. Stir occasionally. Remove the cinnamon stick before serving.

Bread and rice are the staple accompaniments eaten with every single Indian meal. I have included in this chapter detailed cooking instructions for the four best-known types of Indian bread – layered bread (*parathas*), flat bread (*chapatis*), deep-fried puffy bread (*pooris*) and leavened oven bread (*naan*) – all wonderful breads to impress your family and guests.

And if you want to serve rice too, it can be prepared in so many different ways, from simple Spiced Basmati Rice, which beautifully complements many of the savoury dishes in this book, to the delicious Mushroom *Pullao*, a vegetarian meal in itself!

accompaniments

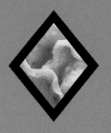

breads

There are all kinds of breads in India, most of them unleavened, eaten in the north at every single meal. Many of these everyday breads are made with a *very* finely ground wholemeal flour that we call *ata*. I find that the British flour that approximates *ata* best is a wheatmeal flour because it has just enough bran in it to give it body without making it too coarse for our soft, pliable breads. Of course, if you have access to Indian grocers and can buy *ata* (sometimes called *chapati* flour) do, by all means, use it.

Some of our breads, such as the *poori*, are deep-fried. The ideal utensil for this is the Indian *karhai* because it is very economical on oil and because it prevents hot oil from splashing on to the cooker. A deep frying-pan may be used as a substitute.

Many other breads are cooked on a *tava*, a concave cast-iron plate that is heated before breads such as *chapatis* and *parathas* are slapped on to it. As I have suggested in the chapter on equipment, a cast-iron frying-pan makes a perfectly adequate substitute.

You will find one other kind of bread in this chapter. It is really a savoury pancake and is made, not with flour but with a split pea (*moong dal*) batter. Such pancakes are a very common breakfast and snack food in India, especially in the west and south.

layered bread

Paratha

We eat these triangular breads frequently with our meals, with vegetables such as Spicy Green Beans (page 132) or Aubergine Cooked in the Pickling Style (page 136) and meats such as Chicken with Cream (page 98).

Makes 12 parathas

175 g (6 oz) sieved wheatmeal flour
185 g (6½ oz) plain flour plus some extra for dusting
½ teaspoon salt
About 10 tablespoons vegetable oil, or melted *ghee* (page 28)
150–200 ml (5–7 fl oz) water

Put the 2 flours and salt in a bowl. Dribble 2 tablespoons of the oil or melted *ghee* over the top. Rub the oil in with your fingertips until the mixture resembles coarse breadcrumbs. Slowly add 150–200 ml (5–7 fl oz) water and gather the flour together to form a softish ball.

Empty the ball on to a clean work surface. Knead for about 10 minutes or until you have a smooth, soft, but not sticky, dough. Form a ball. Rub the ball with about ¼ teaspoon of the oil and slip it into a polythene bag for 30 minutes or longer.

Set a large, cast-iron frying-pan over medium-low heat. Meanwhile, knead the dough again and form 12 equal balls. Keep 11 of them covered while you work with the twelfth. Flatten this ball and dust it with some plain flour. Roll it out into a 15 cm (6 inch) round, dusting your work surface with flour whenever necessary. Spread ¼ teaspoon of the oil over the surface of the *paratha* and fold it in half. Spread about ⅛ teaspoon of the oil over the surface of the half that is on top and fold it into half again to form a triangle. Roll out this triangle into a larger triangle with 18 cm (7 inch) sides. Dust with flour whenever necessary.

Brush the hot frying-pan with ¼ teaspoon of the oil and slap the *paratha* on to it. Let the *paratha* cook for a minute. Now brush the top generously with 1 teaspoon oil. The brushing will take about 30 seconds. Turn the *paratha* over and cook the second side for a minute or so. Both sides should have reddish-gold spots. Move the *paratha* around so all ends are exposed evenly to the heat. Put the cooked *paratha* on a plate. Cover either with an inverted plate or with a piece of aluminium foil. Make all the *parathas* this way.

If *parathas* are not to be eaten right away, wrap them tightly in foil. The whole bundle of *parathas* may then be heated in a 200°C/400°F/Gas 6 oven for 15–20 minutes.

moong dal pancakes with peas

Gujerati poore

Savoury pancakes made out of split peas, or rice and split peas, provide much of India with a nourishing snack food. These protein-rich pancakes are also eaten by many vegetarian Indians at breakfast, usually accompanied by a chutney and a glass of fresh buttermilk. You could also serve them with tea.

Makes about 9 pancakes

185 g (6½ oz) *moong dal*, picked over, washed and drained

1 litre (1¾ pints) plus 85 ml (3 fl oz) plus 1 tablespoon water

50 g (2 oz) shelled peas

2.5 cm (1 inch) cube ginger, peeled and coarsely chopped

2–3 cloves garlic, peeled

1–2 fresh, hot green chillies, cut into 4 pieces each

1 teaspoon salt

¼ teaspoon ground turmeric

50 g (2 oz) onion, peeled and minced

2 tablespoons finely chopped, fresh green coriander

¼ teaspoon bicarbonate of soda

About 120 ml (4 fl oz) vegetable oil

Put the *dal* in a bowl. Add 1 litre (1¾ pints) water and soak for 5 hours. Drain.

Drop the peas into boiling water for 3–4 minutes or until they are tender. Drain and chop coarsely.

Combine the ginger, garlic, green chillies, salt, turmeric, *dal* and 85 ml (3 fl oz) plus 1 tablespoon water in the container of an electric blender. Blend until you have a smooth batter. Let the machine run for 2–3 minutes more so the batter gets light and airy.

Empty the batter into a bowl. Add the onion and fresh coriander and peas. Mix. The batter may now be covered and refrigerated, if you like, for up to 24 hours. Just before you get ready to cook, add the bicarbonate of soda and mix it in. Remember to stir the batter before you make each pancake.

Brush a 20 cm (8 inch) non-stick frying-pan with about 1 teaspoon of the oil and set it over medium-low heat. Remove about 55 ml (2 fl oz) of batter. When the oil is hot, drop this batter right in the centre of the pan. Now, place the rounded bottom of a soup spoon on the centre of the blob of batter. Using a gentle but continuous spiral motion, spread the batter outwards with the back of the spoon, smoothing out any ridges along the way. Make a pancake that is about 14–15 cm (5½–6 inches) in diameter. Dribble a teaspoon of oil over the pancake and another ½ teaspoon around its edges. Cover the pan and let the pancake cook for 2 minutes or until its underside turns a reddish colour. Uncover the pan and turn the pancake over. Cook the pancake on the second side for 1½ minutes or until it develops small red spots. Remove the pancake and put it on a plate. Cover with a second plate, inverted over the first. Make all the pancakes this way, making sure you stir the batter each time.

These pancakes are best eaten hot, just as soon as they are made. You could, if you wish, stack them on a sheet of aluminium foil and then wrap them into a bundle. The whole bundle can be heated in an oven at 220°C/425°F/Gas 7 for 15 minutes.

rice

My Western friends are always telling me that they cannot cook rice. They can hardly be blamed for their phobia. It starts, I think, with inadequate – inaccurate, in fact – instructions on rice packets that invariably suggest using far more water than rice really requires. The rice ends up by being mushy and the people who are cooking it often think that it is their fault. It is not.

There are, actually, many methods of cooking rice well. You will find several in the chapter that follows. Rice can be cooked like pasta, in a lot of boiling water until it is half done. Then it can be drained and 'dried off' in a slow oven. Rice can be cooked completely on top of the cooker with just the correct amount of water needed for absorption. Or you can start cooking rice on top of the cooker with just the amount of water needed for absorption and then finish it off in the oven. The method you choose depends upon the recipe and what you want the rice to do.

If you are unsure about cooking rice, just follow my recipes carefully and you should not go wrong.

There are a few things that are worth remembering when cooking rice.

1 Use a heavy pan with a very tight-fitting lid. If you have a tin-lined copper pan hanging decoratively in your kitchen, this is your chance to use it. An enamelled, cast-iron pan is also good for rice. I find that such pans generally have fairly loose-fitting lids. There is a very quick remedy for this. Just cover the pan tightly with a sheet of aluminium foil first and then with its own lid. You can also make good rice in heavy, stainless-steel pans. Any time you are unsure about the fitting of the lid, interpose a layer of aluminium foil between it and the pan. Be sure to crinkle the edges of the foil so that hardly any steam escapes. In many of my recipes, the rice ends up by cooking in steam. If too much of it escapes, the rice will not cook properly.

2 For best results, rice should be washed in several changes of water and then soaked for about 30 minutes before it is cooked. The washing gets rid of the starchy powder left over from the milling process. The soaking lets each grain absorb water so it sticks less to the next grain while it is cooking.

3 If you are cooking rice with just enough water or stock needed for absorption, what is the correct proportion of liquid to rice? I like to measure my rice in a clear measuring jug and I never use more than 1½ parts liquid to 1 part rice. If I have soaked the rice, my ratio changes to 1⅓ parts liquid to 1 part rice.

4 Sometimes I sauté my rice before I add liquid to it. This also helps to keep the grains separate. When you sauté rice, do it gently. Some types of rice grains, such as basmati, are very delicate, particularly after they have been soaked. If you sauté too vigorously, the grains break up into small pieces.

5 Once I have covered my rice pan with a lid, I like to cook it on very, very low heat. If you cannot adjust your heat very, very low, use an ovenproof pan to begin with, cover it tightly as instructed, and pop it into a pre-heated 170°C/325°F/Gas 3 oven for 25 minutes.

6 Resist any urge you may have to peep into a covered pan of rice before the cooking time is over. Precious steam will escape and the rice will cook unevenly.

7 If you have a thin layer of rice at the top of your pan that does not get cooked all the way through, while the rest of the rice does, then your lid is not tight enough. Use aluminium foil between the pan and the lid next time around. Meanwhile, salvage your present situation by gently covering the partially cooked rice at the top with some fully cooked rice from the bottom. Add a tablespoon or two of water to the pan, cover tightly, this time using the foil, and cook for another 10 minutes over very low heat.

8 When removing cooked rice from the pan, use a large slotted spoon. Either scrape out the rice gently, layer by layer, or else ease the spoon gently into the rice, lift out as much as you can, put it on a plate and then break up any lumps by pressing lightly with the back of the spoon.

rice and peas

Tahiri

This rice dish is flavoured, very mildly, with cumin seeds, making it suitable for almost any kind of meal.

Serves 6

Long-grain rice measured to the 450 ml (15 fl oz) level in a glass measuring jug

1.2 litres (2 pints) plus 600 ml (1 pint) water

3 tablespoons vegetable oil

1 teaspoon cumin seeds

75 g (3 oz) onions, peeled and finely chopped

150–175 g (5–6 oz) fresh, shelled peas (frozen, defrosted peas may be substituted)

1 teaspoon salt

Wash the rice in several changes of water and drain. Put the rice in a bowl. Add 1.2 litres (2 pints) water and soak for 30 minutes. Drain.

Put the oil in a heavy pan and set over medium heat. When hot, put in the cumin seeds. Stir them about for 3 seconds. Now put in the chopped onions. Stir and fry them until they get flecked with brown spots. Add the peas, rice and salt. Stir and sauté gently for 3–4 minutes or until the peas and rice are coated with oil. Add 600 ml (1 pint) water and bring to a boil. Cover very tightly, turn heat to very, very low and cook for 25 minutes. Turn off the heat and let the pan sit, covered and undisturbed, for another 5 minutes. Stir gently before serving.

lamb and rice casserole
Mughlai lamb biryani

Biryanis are grand, festive casseroles in which partially cooked rice is layered over cooked meat. Orange saffron milk is dribbled over the top, thereby colouring some grains yellow while leaving others white, and the dish set to bake in a slow oven. As it cooks, the *biryani* gets quite perfumed with saffron.

Saffron is expensive and many people, even in India, use yellow food colouring as a substitute. Just use 1 teaspoon yellow liquid food colouring diluted with 1 teaspoon water instead of the saffron and warm milk. Soaking the rice in salted water for 3–24 hours, is an ancient trick the Persians used to get rice grains as white – and as separate from each other – as possible.

A *biryani* is really a meal in itself and may be eaten with just a yoghurt dish, such as Yoghurt with Aubergines (page 212), and a relish, such as my Tomato, Onion and Green Coriander Relish (page 215). However, *biryanis* are generally served at feasts and banquets when it would not be at all amiss to serve these condiments *as well as* Chicken in a Red Sweet Pepper Sauce (page 101) and Cauliflower with Onion and Tomato (page 142).

We like to perk up our meals in India with a variety of condiments. Their function, apart from teasing the palate with their sharp contrasts of sweet, sour, hot and salty flavours, is to balance out the meal with added protein and vitamins.

Sometimes, these condiments can be quite simple – cucumber wedges seasoned quickly with salt, pepper, cayenne and lemon juice or chopped-up onions and tomatoes. At other times we can serve pickles that have taken weeks or months to mature. Some condiments, such as the Fresh Coriander Chutney or the Gujerati Carrot Salad, should be eaten up within 48 hours. Others, such as the Apple, Peach and Apricot Chutney and the Cauliflower and White Radish Pickle, may be kept for a year.

Yoghurt relishes fall into another category. They can be condiments or they can be substantial dishes by themselves. Almost any herb or vegetable can be put into yoghurts, from mint to potatoes. Whenever I am serving an all-Indian meal, I nearly always serve a yoghurt relish because it provides a cooling contrast.

relishes, chutneys and pickles

plain yoghurt

Dahi

Yoghurt is used in India for marinating meats – it tenderizes them – as a tart, creamy flavouring and as an ingredient for sauces. As it is rich in protein, it is also eaten at almost every meal, either plain or mixed with seasonings and vegetables. It is a food that is easy to digest, far easier than milk. It is also considered a food that 'settles' the stomach, especially when combined with plain rice.

Naturally, few respectable Indian homes are ever without it. Most of the time it is made at home, although it can be bought from the bazaar as well.

To make yoghurt at home, you need milk, either whole or fat-free, and some 'starter'. This 'starter' is a few tablespoons of borrowed, left-over or bought yoghurt. You also need a warm temperature that hovers between 30°–38°C (85°–100°F). This is the temperature at which yoghurt sets best. As this is not normally room temperature, it has to be approximated. You could put the yoghurt in a warm cupboard near the water heater or in the oven of a cooker with a pilot light. The yoghurt bowl is also quite amenable to being wrapped in a blanket. I frequently resort to the blanket method.

1 litre (1³/₄ pints) milk
2 tablespoons natural yoghurt

Bring the milk to a boil in a heavy pan. As soon as the milk begins to rise, remove the pan from the cooker. Let the milk cool to anywhere between 38° and 43°C (100–110°F). It should feel warm to the touch. If a film forms over the top, stir it in.

Put the yoghurt in a 1.2 litre (2 pint) stainless-steel or non-metallic bowl and beat it with a whisk until it is smooth and creamy. Slowly, add the warm milk, a little bit at a time and stirring as you do so. Cover the bowl and then wrap it in an old blanket or shawl without tilting it. Set it aside in a warm place free of draughts for 6–8 hours, or until the yoghurt has set.

Store the yoghurt in a refrigerator. It should stay fresh for 4–5 days.

yoghurt with aubergines

Baigan ka raita

Here is a soothing, cooling and exceedingly simple way to serve aubergines. I like to serve this with Delhi-style Lamb Cooked with Potatoes (page 73), Gujerati-style Green Beans (page 131) and either rice or an Indian bread.

Serves 6

1 medium-sized (550 g/1¼ lb) aubergine, peeled and cut into 2.5 cm (1 inch) cubes

600 ml (1 pint) natural yoghurt

¾ teaspoon salt, or to taste

Freshly ground black pepper

⅛ teaspoon cayenne pepper (optional)

1 spring onion, washed and cut into paper-thin rounds all the way up its green section

1 tablespoon finely chopped, fresh mint

A few mint leaves for garnishing

Bring water in the bottom part of a steaming utensil to the boil. (If you do not have a steaming utensil, set a steaming trivet or a colander inside a large pan. Pour water into the pan in such a way that it stays just below the lowest part of the trivet or colander. Bring this water to a boil.)

Put the aubergine cubes into the steamer section of your steaming utensil (or into the trivet or colander), cover and steam over high heat for 10 minutes. Make sure that your boiling water does not run out.

While the aubergine is steaming, put the yoghurt into a bowl and beat it lightly with a fork or a whisk until it is smooth and creamy. Add the salt, black pepper, cayenne, if using, spring onion and mint to it. Mix with a fork.

Lift out the steamed aubergine pieces and mash with a fork. Spread out the aubergine on a plate and leave to cool somewhat (or else the yoghurt would curdle).

Fold the aubergine into the yoghurt and garnish with mint leaves.

spicy cucumber wedges

Kheere ke tukray

These wedges (pictured opposite) are refreshing and deliciously crunchy and may be served with any Indian meal. It is best to prepare them at the last minute, just before you sit down to eat.

Serves 4

275 g (10 oz) cucumber
(about 25 cm/10 inches)

$1/3$ teaspoon salt

$1/8$ teaspoon cayenne pepper

Freshly ground black pepper

$1/3$ teaspoon ground, roasted cumin seeds
(page 20)

Juice of $3/4$ lemon (approx.)

Peel the cucumber and cut it into half, crosswise. Now cut each half into 4 sections, lengthwise. Arrange the wedges on a plate. Sprinkle the salt, cayenne, black pepper, ground, roasted cumin seeds and lemon juice over them. **Serve immediately**.

fresh coriander chutney

Hare dhaniye ki chutney

This is the kind of chutney that is made fresh in our homes every day. We eat small amounts – 1–2 teaspoons – with our meals, just as you might eat mustard with sausages. It also serves as an excellent dip for snacks such as *samosas*.

Serves 4–6

75 g (3 oz) fresh green coriander
(weight without lower stems and roots),
coarsely chopped

$1/2$–1 fresh, hot green chilli,
coarsely chopped

$1^1/2$ tablespoons lemon juice

$1/2$ teaspoon salt

$1/2$ teaspoon ground, roasted cumin seeds
(page 20)

Freshly ground black pepper

Combine all the ingredients in the container of an electric blender. Blend, pushing down with a rubber spatula several times, until you have a paste. Empty the paste into a small glass or other non-metallic bowl.

Everyday meals in India generally end with fresh fruit – mangoes, pineapples, oranges, apples, pears, bananas, guavas, cherries, loquats, melons, jack-fruit – whatever happens to be in season. Fruit is refreshing and cleansing – and a perfect conclusion to a spicy meal.

In our family, my mother always peeled and cut the smaller fruit for all of us at the table. A plate was passed around and we took what we wanted. Larger, messier fruit, such as watermelons, were cut in the kitchen before the meal and left to cool in the refrigerator.

Desserts and sweetmeats are usually reserved for festive occasions. A wedding banquet invariably brings forth large vats filled with *kulfi* – Indian ice-cream – and at religious festivals some variety of *halva* is nearly always served.

sweets

drunken orange slices
Sharabi narangi

There could be nothing simpler than this dessert. All that it requires are good oranges,
some cinnamon and Grand Marnier. It is just perfect after a spicy Indian meal.

Serves 4

4 good, juicy oranges
1/3 teaspoon ground cinnamon
120 ml (4 fl oz) Grand Marnier

Peel the whole oranges, leaving no white pith. Slice into 5 mm (1/4 inch) thick
rounds and arrange in a bowl in overlapping slices, sprinkling a little cinnamon
over each layer. Cover and refrigerate. Just before serving, pour the Grand
Marnier evenly over the top.

ice-cream with nuts

Kulfi

As far as I can remember, we never made *kulfi* at home. This may well have been because it was served always to hundreds of people at wedding banquets. Only a professional *kulfi-wallah* could be entrusted with such a monstrous task. Orders were placed with him weeks in advance. On the day of the banquet, he arrived with assistants, usually his sons and brothers, carrying enormous earthenware vats. The vats were set up somewhere outdoors, usually at the edge of a vast lawn. Each vat contained lots of broken ice and, embedded in the ice, hundreds of tube-shaped terracotta containers filled with *kulfi*. Every now and then the *kulfi-wallah* would ease his arm into the vats and give its contents a knowing swish. *Kulfi* is not difficult to make at home as I have discovered in the years that I have been deprived of local *kulfi-wallahs*. All you need is an adequate freezer. (If you have an ice-cream machine, you may use it for *kulfi*.) *Kulfi* is not made with cream but with reduced milk. It helps to have a very heavy pan with an even distribution of heat for boiling down the milk. A heavy, non-stick pan would also do.

Serves 6

2 litres (3½ pints) milk
10 cardamom pods
4–5 tablespoons sugar
15 g (½ oz) chopped, blanched almonds
25 g (1 oz) chopped, unsalted pistachios

Bring the milk to a boil in a heavy pan. As soon as the milk begins to rise, turn the heat down, adjusting it to allow the milk to simmer vigorously without boiling over. Add the cardamom pods. The milk has to reduce to about a third of its original amount, that is, to about 750 ml (1¼ pints). Stir frequently as this happens. Whenever a film forms on top of the milk, just stir it in.

When the milk has reduced, remove the cardamom pods and discard them. Add the sugar and almonds. Stir and simmer gently for 2–3 minutes. Pour the reduced milk into a bowl and let it cool completely. Add half of the pistachios and stir them in. Cover the bowl with aluminium foil and put it in the freezer. (If you have an ice-cream machine, you could empty the contents of the bowl into the machine and get it going.)

Put 6 small, individual cups, empty yoghurt cartons or a 900 ml (1½ pint) pudding basin into the freezer.

Every 15 minutes or so, remove the ice-cream bowl from the freezer and give the ice-cream a good stir in order to break up the crystals. As the ice-cream begins to freeze, it will become harder and harder to stir it. When it becomes almost impossible to stir, take the containers out of the freezer. Work quickly now. Divide the ice-cream between the cups or empty it into the pudding basin. Sprinkle the remaining pistachios over the top. Cover the cups or basin with aluminium foil, crinkling the edges to seal them. Put into the freezer and let the ice-cream harden.

carrot halva

Gajar ka halva

This is a lovely, fresh-tasting halva that makes the most of the natural sweetness
of carrots.

Serves 4

450 g (1 lb) carrots

750 ml (1¼ pints) milk

8 cardamom pods

5 tablespoons vegetable oil or *ghee* (page 28)

5 tablespoons caster sugar

1–2 tablespoons sultanas

1 tablespoon shelled, unsalted pistachios, lightly crushed

300 ml (10 fl oz) clotted or double cream (optional)

Peel the carrots and grate them either by hand or in a food processor. Put the grated carrots, milk and cardamom pods in a heavy-bottomed pan and bring to a boil. Turn heat to medium and cook, stirring now and then, until there is no liquid left. Adjust the heat, if you need to. This boiling down of the milk will take you at least 30 minutes or longer, depending upon the width of your pan.

Put the oil or *ghee* in a non-stick frying-pan and set over medium-low heat. When hot, put in the carrot mixture. Stir and fry until the carrots no longer have a wet, milky look. They should turn a rich, reddish colour. This can take 10–15 minutes.

Add the sugar, sultanas and pistachios. Stir and fry another 2 minutes.

This *halva* may be served warm or at room temperature.

Serve the cream on the side for those who want it.

creamy rice pudding

Phirni

As a child, there was nothing more comforting to me than to come home from school and find shallow terracotta bowls of this creamy dessert cooling in neat rows in the refrigerator, all lightly dusted with slivers of pistachios and almonds. Even though they were meant to be eaten at the end of the evening meal, my mother always filled extra individual bowls so that we could eat their contents as a quick snack.

Since the milk needs to be reduced somewhat, I like to use a wide pan – non-stick is ideal – which allows for quicker evaporation.

Serves 4–6

1 litre (1³/₄ pints) rich milk

10 cardamom pods

3 tablespoons finely ground rice

6–7 tablespoons sugar

4 tablespoons slivered, blanched almonds

2 tablespoons finely slivered or finely chopped unsalted pistachios

Pour the milk into a wide, preferably non-stick, pan. Add the cardamom pods and bring to a boil without letting the milk spill over. Quickly turn heat to medium – the milk should simmer as vigorously as possible without boiling over – and cook, stirring now and then, for about 15–20 minutes or until the milk has reduced to 750 ml (1¼ pints).

Sprinkle the ground rice slowly into the pan, stirring as you go. Add the sugar as well. Cook, stirring now and then, for 7–8 minutes or until the pudding has thickened to a creamy consistency, turning the heat down a bit towards the end of this cooking time. Turn off the heat. Pick out and discard the cardamom pods.

Set a small, cast-iron frying-pan over medium heat. When very hot, put in the almonds. Stir, shake or toss them until they are lightly roasted and turn golden. Set them aside.

Put the pistachios into the same hot frying-pan and roast them even more briefly until they turn just a shade darker. Set aside.

When the pudding has cooled to lukewarm, stir the almonds into it. Ladle the pudding into 4–6 small ramekin dishes. Sprinkle the top with the pistachios and cover with cling film. Refrigerate for 2–3 hours until cold and set.

mangoes

Good mangoes are amongst the best fruit on earth. They can be found in two basic forms, tinned and fresh. The tinned ones come sliced, or as a purée. I rarely serve the slices as I find their texture to be pathetically mushy but I do use the purée. I often chill it thoroughly, then swirl it into a bowl filled with double the amount of whipped cream and sprinkle some toasted almonds or pistachios over the top. It is a very simple dessert. Very refreshing too.

Fresh mangoes are another matter. If you ever see good ones (those with a strong mango aroma), such as the *alphonso* from the Bombay region, do buy them. Remember, though, that many grocers sell mangoes that are not fully ripe. Such mangoes may be ripened at home. Just wrap them individually in newspaper and then put them in a covered basket or cardboard box. Leave this container in a warm place (such as the kitchen) until the mangoes are ripe. A ripe mango should yield slightly when pressed. After the mangoes have ripened, they should be chilled, peeled and sliced. Mangoes do have stones. So you have to slice around them. Do not throw the stones away before nibbling off all the flesh first!